SERIES EDITOR: LEE JOHNSON

OSPREY MILITARY WARRIOR SERIES: 20

BRITISH REDCOAT (2)
1793-1815

TEXT BY
STUART REID

COLOUR BY
GRAHAM TURNER

OSPREY
MILITARY

D1300744

First published in Great Britain in 1997 by Osprey, a division of
Reed Consumer Books Ltd. Michelin House, 81 Fulham Road,
London SW3 6RB and Auckland, Melbourne, Singapore and Toronto.

ISBN 1 85532 556 X

Military Editor: Iain MacGregor
Design: The Black Spot

Filmset in Great Britain
Printed through World Print Ltd., Hong Kong

*For a catalogue of all books published by
Osprey Military please write to:*

The Marketing Manager, Consumer Catalogue Department,
Osprey Publishing Ltd, Michelin House, 81 Fulham Road,
London SW3 6RB

Dedication and thanks

To the 68th (Durham) Light Infantry display group.

Acknowledgements

Susan Benneworth who was kind enough to photograph the posed
shots of the reenactors.

Artist's note

Readers may care to note the original paintings from which the colour
plates in this book were prepared are available for private sale. All
reproduction copyright whatsoever is retained by the publisher.
Enquiries should be addressed to:

'Five Acres', Buslins Lane, Chartridge, Bucks, HP5 2SN.

The publishers regret that they can enter into no correspondence
upon this matter.

Publisher's note

Readers may wish to study this title in conjunction with the following
Osprey publications:

MAA 39 *British Army in North America 1775-1801*
MAA 48 *Wolfe's Army*
MAA 114 *Wellington's Infantry: (1)*
MAA 118 *The Jacobite Rebellions 1689-1745*
MAA 119 *Wellington's Infantry: (2)*
MAA 141 *Napoleon's Line Infantry*
MAA 146 *Napoleon's Light Infantry*
MAA 153 *Napoleon's Guard Infantry: (1)*
MAA 160 *Napoleon's Guard Infantry: (2)*
MAA 199 *Napoleon's Specialist Troops*
MAA 204 *Wellington's Specialist Troops*
MAA 211 *Napoleon's Overseas Army*
MAA 224 *French Army in the American War of Independence*
MAA 226 *The American War 1812-14*
MAA 244 *French Army in the American War of Independence*
MAA 273 *General Washington's Army: (1) 1775-1778*
MAA 285 *King George's Army 1740-93: (1)*
MAA 289 *King George's Army 1740-93: (2)*
MAA 290 *General Washington's Army: (2) 1778-1783*
MAA 292 *King George's Army 1740-93: 3*
MAA 294 *British Forces in the West Indies 1792-1815*
MAA 296 *Louis XV's Army: (1) Heavy Cavalry & Dragoons*
WAR 19 *British Redcoat: (1) 1740-1793*
Elite 52 *Wellington's Foot Guards*
CAM 12 *Culloden 1746*
CAM 15 *Waterloo 1815*
CAM 28 *New Orleans 1815*
CAM 37 *Boston 1775*

BRITISH REDCOAT (2) 1793-1815

Volunteers Wanted,

For General FRASER's Highland Regiment, to consist of two Battalions, the greatest part of which are already raised.

This is to give notice to all gentlemen Volunteers, who are able and willing to serve his Majesty *King George*, that *Ensign Thomas Hamilton*, in said regiment, has opened a rendezvous at *Dundee*, (at Mrs Carmichael's), *Perth*, *Dunkeld*, and *Pittenweem*, where Volunteers will be immediately received. His stay will be short in this country, as he goes south in March next, to deliver over his men to the regiment. Persons, therefore, willing to enter into this regiment, (which holds forth such lucrative terms) will do well not to miss this opportunity. *No price will be grudged* for good men, who will (besides the bounty-money) enter into present pay and good quarters. The advantages that will arise to those who inlist into this *corps*, are very great. They are to go to *America*, and by his *Majesty's royal* and *most gracious proclamation*, they will be intitled to a *full discharge* at the end of *three years, that is in 1779*, or of the present *American rebellion*. Now, considering that the British army will be from forty to fifty thousand men strong, there, in spring next, it cannot, in all human probability, fail to be entirely quelled, next summer. Then, gentlemen, will be your *harvest*, and the best one too you ever cropt. You will, each of you, by visiting this *new world*, become the *founders of families*. The lands of the *rebels* will be divided amongst you, and every one of you become *lairds*. No old regiment will have such advantages. Is not this better than starving at home in these poor times? and will a man of spirit sit unmoved, and hear such proffered terms? Ye who are now dreading the sentence of *stool-meal*, who are drudging like slaves under a *cruel* or *harsh task-master*. Any of you who have got a *termagant* or *cross wife*, or who smart under the displeasure of an *ungracious parent*, come all to *Ensign Thomas Hamilton*, and he will ease your fears, and make you at once free and happy.

Dundee, Jan. 8. 1776.   *GOD save the KING.*

Recruiting poster; although dating from 1776, this is a very typical example of the appeal made to recruits throughout this period. While the promise of land was an obvious incentive, the real attractions are spelt out at the end. (National Museums of Scotland)

INTRODUCTION

This book is the second of two volumes covering the British infantryman between 1740 and 1815. The first volume, *The British Redcoat 1740-1793*, deals with life in the 18th century army and the development of infantry tactics up to and including the American War, 1775-83. This volume takes the story forward to Waterloo.

In 1783 the British army came straggling home from North America in what can only be described as a shattered condition. It had invariably acquitted itself well on the battlefield, but its regiments were now woefully under-strength, and it was not until 1789 that they were once again fit for service. Little more than three years later, in February 1793, Republican France declared war, and apart from two short periods amounting to no more than a few months apiece, the army was to be heavily engaged in a series of campaigns around the globe for the next 23 years.

RECRUITMENT

Throughout the 18th century the British army relied for the most part upon each regiment sending out small parties of officers and men to 'drum up' for volunteers. This process was quite straightforward, and is discussed in greater detail in The British Redcoat (Warrior 19), but the quite unprecedented demand for men in the 1790s placed considerable strains upon it, particularly since it appears that the post of Inspector General of Recruiting was vacant from 1791 until 1795 and in 1806 then merged with that of Adjutant General.

Leaving aside the footguards, there were just 77 numbered regiments of the line at the outbreak of war in February 1793. Of these, only the 1st (Royal) Regiment and 60th (Royal American) Regiment had more than one battalion. Moreover, most units were already committed to Imperial defence, and relatively few were available for immediate operations.

More troops were urgently required, and at the stroke of a pen the authorised establishment of the existing units was more than doubled,

Highlanders at West Barns Camp, East Lothian. Note the stag which is presumably serving as a regimental mascot. (NMS)

from 370 rank and file to 850. Although increasing the size of existing units rather than raising completely new ones might have seemed the more efficient course of action, the effectiveness of this measure was quite limited, since it was extremely difficult for units stationed overseas to find the required new recruits in the first place. A typical example was 1/Royals, who despite being stationed on Jamaica since early 1790 had more or less succeeded in maintaining their strength at the old establishment. Suddenly they needed to recruit an additional 480 men, but as the records show, only three men for the battalion were embarked on the *Arnold and Polly* on 10 October and 74 on the *Ulysses* on 19 November 1793. Moreover, apart from two local men enlisted on San Domingo, the only recruits to be received in 1794 were a draft of 39 men embarked on the *Lively* on 19 September.

In the circumstances, it is hardly surprising that the Government promptly fell back on the deceptively simple expedient of raising new regiments. Between March 1793 and the summer of 1795, no fewer than 81 battalions were raised, including 58 battalions of the line numbered from the 78th (Seaforth) Highlanders to the 135th Loyal Irish Volunteers, together with a further 15 unnumbered battalions that bore titles such as the Scotch Brigade (three battalions) and the Royal Glasgow Regiment of Foot, and eight second battalions for some new and existing units. Almost without exception, these new units were 'raised for rank', meaning that the officers were obliged to find a certain number of recruits within a specified time in order to earn permanent commissions. In some cases, where a local corporation pledged its support or the prospective colonel took a more than ordinary interest in the corps, the results were excellent, particularly when enhanced bounties were offered. All too often, however, the desperate need to find the required quota of men produced some very poor recruits indeed.

Similarly, albeit on a smaller scale, the raising of independent companies was sanctioned. Once again the officers concerned entered into agreements with the Government to raise a specified number of men. In return they would be given a corresponding permanent commission in the army. The roots of this system went back to mediaeval times, but while an old-style mercenary captain was expected to lead his independent (or 'free') company off to war, his late 18th century counterpart had no sooner completed his company than the personnel were drafted into larger units and officers who could not be assimilated were placed on half pay.

In terms of numbers, if not quality, the 1794 recruiting drive was a considerable success. The problem was redistributing the raw material to where it would do most good. The older regiments had, of course, been quite unable to meet their new manpower targets, either by their own efforts or through the time honoured practice of occasionally taking drafts of men from newer units. Yet it was these supposedly battle-worthy units who stood in greatest need of augmentation. The Government therefore decided, in the summer of 1795, to take the drastic step of 'reducing' all of those numbered and unnumbered regiments junior to the then 100th Foot. Recruiting for these units was to be suspended, and all their enlisted personnel were drafted into selected low numbered units.

Unpopular as it was, the process should have been straightforward enough, but in the event the cuts went far deeper. With the exception of the 98th (Argyllshire) and 100th (Gordon) Highlanders, all the regiments junior to the 90th Foot, together with the newly raised second battalions of the 2nd, 25th, 29th, 69th, 78th, 82nd, 84th and 90th Foot, were also drafted out of existence by the end of the century. Pigot's 130th Foot escaped this massacre only to be quite literally wiped out by Yellow Fever on San Domingo: on 1 November 1795 it had mustered 166 rank and file fit for duty; exactly a month later it had just seven, with a further 11 in hospital!

In some instances the personnel from these 'reduced' battalions were scattered far and wide, but for the most part they were turned over *en masse* to a single unit. The short-lived 2/25th, for example, was drafted in its entirety into the 31st Foot, while the 2/78th were rather more happily absorbed into the 1/78th, and the Scotch Brigade, the only one of the unnumbered units to survive, was reduced from three battalions to one and eventually designated the 94th Foot. Generally speaking, there appears to have been a conscious attempt to draft men from one Scottish unit into another, but it did not always work: Hay's 109th (Aberdeenshire) Highlanders turned over their personnel to the 53rd (Shropshire) Regiment, while the men of Montgomerie's Royal Glasgow Regiment went into the 44th (East Essex) Regiment.

Welcome though these drafts were to the old regiments, it was obviously a one-off bounty, and radical measures needed to be taken to improve the flow of new recruits. One measure introduced that same year was the establishment of recruiting districts, of which there were 15

Private, 3rd Footguards, by Dayes c1791. This essentially was the field-service uniform and equipment worn by all British infantry (with the exception of Highland corps) at the beginning of the great war with France. Note how the knapsack has two breast-straps. (NMS)

in England, four in Scotland and five in Ireland. Each was presided over by an inspecting field officer with an adjutant, sergeant major and 'requisite number of depot sergeants'. In the following year a 'hospital mate' was added to the staff of each district in order to examine the recruits medically.

At the same time, in September 1795, the authorised establishment of the old battalions was revised downwards to a more realistic level. Now they were to muster only 570 rank and file, but were at the same time augmented by two 'additional' or recruiting companies which could contain up to a total of 110 privates at any one time.

Considerable numbers of men were also being recruited for the fencible regiments, and as substitutes for those balloted to the militia. The former were initially intended to be home defence units and were not to serve overseas – which made them particularly attractive to men scared off from the regulars by the prospect of being sent to the West Indies. Although some fencible regiments did arguably play a vital part in the defence of the realm, their real achievement was simply to soak up men who might otherwise have been signed up for unlimited service in the regular army. Consequently, all those regiments were disbanded between 1798 and 1802, and on the renewed outbreak of war in 1803, the experiment was not repeated. Instead most (though not all) regiments of the line were authorised to raise second battalions.

This two-battalion system was quite different from that previously employed, and to some extent it foreshadowed the Cardwell reforms. The 1st (Royal) Regiment had maintained two battalions throughout the 18th century, but although they bore the same title, wore the same uniform and had the same colonel, they were to all intents and purposes quite independent units. Now, however, it was intended that the new second battalions would serve primarily as depot units, remaining at home and feeding drafts of recruits to their first battalions, while at the same time remaining available for local defence or the policing duties habitually required of army units. In practice the demands for men were so great that many of the second battalions actually proceeded to active service, sometimes replacing or even serving alongside their first battalions.

In order to raise the second battalions, the Government reluctantly authorised the recruiting of militiamen (see **Plate A**). The regular army had been casting covetous eyes on the militia for some time, and

Although simply captioned "A Sergeant of Infantry", this splendid looking figure by Bunbury must surely be a Sergeant Major. (NMS)

North Barrack Block, Fort George Ardersier. Although designed and built in the 1750s, this establishment has been in continuous use by the army ever since, and served as a model for the large-scale barrack building programme of the 1790s. (Author)

sporadic attempts had already been made to take them on active service. Some of the early experiments with light infantry had been carried out using provisional battalions made up of militia flank companies, and in 1799 considerable numbers of militiamen had volunteered for service in Holland. The results had been somewhat mixed but the precedent had been established, and between 1805 and 1814 some 100,000 of them volunteered for service in the regulars.

The great advantage of taking volunteers from the militia was that instead of the small trickle of volunteers gathered in by conventional recruiting parties, they tended to come in large contingents – measured in double or even treble figures – and what's more were already properly trained. Calling for individual volunteers was one thing, but the employment of militia battalions overseas was still contrary to the Militia Acts. Nevertheless a militia brigade (made up of three provisional battalions) was eventually sent out to join Wellington's army in 1814, only to arrive too late to take part in the fighting.

THE SOLDIERS

A fairly typical picture of the average infantryman is provided by the attestation papers for recruits for the 100th (Gordon) Highlanders when it was first raised, in 1794. The average age of the privates was 23, with the youngest being a boy of nine named Robert Watt and the oldest being 47. This compares with an inspection report in 1/Royals in 1789, which found that 35% of the rank and file were aged between 20 and 24, while a further 28% were aged between 25 and 29. Only 7% were aged between 35 and 39, and none admitted to being older.

Out of 913 of the original recruits for the 100th, whose previous occupations are recorded, 442 (48.5%) were simply described as "labourers",

Private 92nd (Gordon) Highlanders 1815. This print by a French artist gives a good general impression of a Highland soldier in full marching order. Note particularly the well stiffened pack. As it happens regimental standing orders forbade the use of the peak on the bonnet by soldiers of the 92nd. (NMS)

and 186 (20%) were "weavers". The former category appears to have been something of a catch-all, used to describe any recruit who could not claim any particular trade or calling; the latter, however, was a very common one in the army. Sergeant James Donaldson of the 94th (Scotch Brigade) recalled: "...You could scarce catch a weaver contented. They are always complaining. Therefore you would never have much trouble enticing them to enlist..."

As for the rest of this sample, 42 were tailors, 31 were shoemakers, 20 were woolcombers, 17 were blacksmiths and 13 were wrights (carpenters). The remainder represented no particular group or even social class, but included a china mender, a bookbinder, a gamekeeper, four hatmakers, a bonnetmaker, a sailor, a saddler, two ropemakers, an excise officer and a sheriff officer, a wine cooper and a Chelsea Out-Pensioner. In addition a fair number of other men were either former soldiers or had transferred from other units.

All regiments of the line were authorised to 'beat up' for volunteers anywhere in the British Isles and North America, and they normally did so without paying much attention to the territorial titles awarded after the American War. Irishmen, in particular, were taken on in unprecedented numbers, although it is important to appreciate that casual use of the term 'Irish' can be rather misleading: as far as the army's records were concerned, it merely indicated where a man was born, and made no distinction between say a Scotch-Irish artisan from Belfast, an Anglo-Irish tradesman from Dublin or a Gaelic Irish labourer from County Kerry.

In 1809 19% of the 28th (Worcestershire) Regiment were Irish, as were 37% of the 57th (West Middlesex). These percentages appear to have been fairly typical, although there were some quite remarkable fluctuations. The 68th (Durham) Regiment, having returned from the West Indies in 1798 with a mere 36 rank and file, received no fewer than 1,777 volunteers from the Irish militia in 1799 and temporarily formed a second battalion. Obviously, at this stage, well over 90% of the regiment was Irish, but by 1811, after another period of service in the West Indies, the proportion of Irishmen in the regiment had dropped to 42%, with 47% English and 11% Scots. This alteration was largely the result of drawing substantial blocks of volunteers from the militia rather than simply relying on traditional recruiting parties. Out of 925 recruits enlisted for the 68th between September 1806 and June 1809, 353 were drawn from the Dumfries, South Lincolnshire and Yorkshire West Riding militia regiments and (in a quite exceptional nod towards their notional county connection) a further 168 had volunteered from the Durham militia.

Cosmo Gordon, Captain and Lieutenant Colonel, 3rd Footguards. Although probably dating to about 1780, this portrait provides a useful example of a distinctive style of regimental grenadier cap, which does not conform to the universal pattern prescribed in 1768. (NMS)

In Scotland it was a slightly different story. In 1789 an inspection revealed that 58% of the enlisted personnel in 1/Royals were Scots, 21.5% Irish and 20.5% English. With minor fluctuations up and down, these percentages were broadly maintained throughout the period, despite confirmation of the title 'Royal Scots' in 1812. Highland regiments did, however, tend to be rather more particular about where they found their recruits. When it was first raised, 93% of the 100th/92nd (Gordon) Highlanders were Scots and only 6% Irish, while English and Irish recruits (just 14 in all) together amounted to slightly over 1% of the 78th (Seaforth) Highlanders. On the other hand, in 1799 only 45% of the 79th (Cameron) Highlanders were Scots and another 45% were English, while Irishmen accounted for only 9%. The remaining 1% were 'foreigners'. Similarly, the 73rd were notionally a Highland regiment, but they lost their kilts in 1808 and the second battalion appears to have been very substantially raised from Irish militiamen in the following year. However, by 1815 66% of its personnel were English, as against only 24% who were recorded to have been born in Ireland, and a mere 10% Scots.

ARMY LIFE

"A soldier's life," said Alice, "is terrible hard." Of this there is no doubt, although there is a tendency to paint a far bleaker picture than was actually the case. When not on active service, daily routines centred around training, fatigues and guard duties, as in the modern army. When not thus occupied with duties, the soldier was pretty well left to his own devices, and if the opportunity arose, he could seek part-time work to supplement his army pay.

Sergeant Anton wrote: "During this period the Leith wet-docks were forming, and gave employment to a great number of labourers as well as to soldiers. Such was the demand for willing hands, that not an idle man was to be found in the barracks, while these works were carrying on: all were actively employed, with the exception of those left for the purpose of duty. I was one of the latter class, and considered myself well paid by being allowed to mount guard for some of those at work, when it came to their turn of duty, as they seldom paid less than two shillings for each turn."

This 'moonlighting' was a time honoured practice in the 18th century, and perhaps the most obvious difference in conditions after 1793 was the greatly increased provision of proper barrack accommodation. Except in Ireland, the provision of barrack accommodation had

Port Arms as demonstrated by a member of the 68th (Durham) Light Infantry in light marching order – carrying everything except his knapsack. (Author)

been grossly inadequate throughout the 18th century, and where it did exist it was more of the nature of transit accommodation. The largest barracks in the country, Fort George at Ardersier, had originally been conceived and built as a fire-base in the wake of the last Jacobite rising, with permanent accommodation for two battalions and enough secure space to encamp a third. By the time it was completed, the threat of another rising had receded and throughout its existence the fort served largely as a depot for newly raised regiments (see **Plate F**). Similarly, the largest barracks complex in England, at Chatham, was used primarily for processing recruits intended for regiments serving overseas.

New barrack-building policy

In 1793, however, the position changed quite dramatically with the appointment of Colonel Oliver De Lancey as Barrackmaster General, and over the next two years a massive programme of barrack-building took place. The reasons for this programme were two-fold: in the first place the Home Office was keen to be able to concentrate troops in towns, for police duties; and in the second both the Home Office and the Horse Guards were keen to isolate those troops from the assumed subversive notions of the civil population, upon whom they might oth-

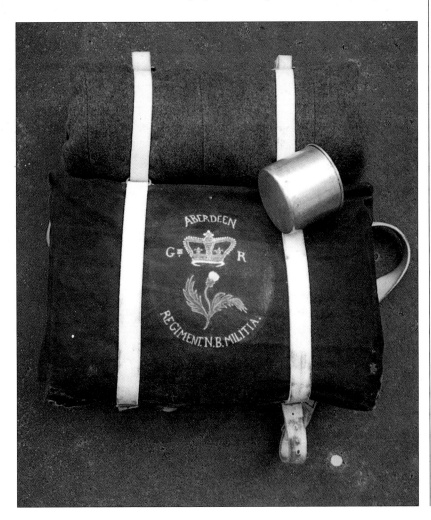

Reconstruction: Envelope or "Trotter" knapsack with the wooden stiffening removed and painted with the badge of the Aberdeenshire Militia. Knapsacks were the soldier's personal property, and there are a number of references to volunteers from the militia continuing to carry knapsacks with militia badges (and often wearing militia uniforms as well) while serving in regular units. (Author)

Charge bayonets demonstrated by a corporal and private of the 68th. Note that only the front rank man actually charges his bayonet while his rear rank man ports arms. (Author)

erwise be billeted. Some of the fencible mutinies in 1794 were certainly attributed to the latter, but the real reason was probably more to do with poor discipline, and placing the men in proper barracks was bound to improve that.

Nevertheless, the barracks were a mixed blessing. The very haste with which they were thrown up, along with the political considerations which governed their siting, generally ensured that they were badly built, far too cramped and often situated in the wrong place. Moreover, supply never caught up with demand, and billeting on the civil population continued to be a feature of army life throughout the period.

With few exceptions, the new barracks could not house more than a single battalion, and whenever it became necessary to concentrate larger bodies of troops (usually prior to shipping them overseas), they would be accommodated instead in large tented camps. One of the largest such concentrations took place on Nursling Common, near Southampton, in the summer of 1795, when a large-scale 'descent' was being planned on the West Indies, with a corresponding concentration of Irish regiments at Cork. Similar temporary camps were periodically established as training camps during the 18th century, and during this period the light infantry training camps at Shornecliffe and Brabourne Lees were notable examples.

Accommodation in the field

Tents were evidently taken to Flanders in 1793, for a memorandum dated 8 January 1794 refers to the need for a complete set of new tents to be sent out in order to replace those already "damaged" on campaign. It requests that they be "the new invented round tents which the brigades of the line have had this campaign and which from experience are found to be infinitely preferable to the old infantry tents". Contemporary military dictionaries state that the 'Flanders Tent', or Bell Tent, as it became more familiarly known, could accommodate 12 men, but in practice it is generally possible to fit only eight men and their equipment comfortably inside.

Most British expeditionary forces thereafter appear to have used bell tents, except in the Peninsula, where Wellington tried to do without tents at all, relying instead on billeting and makeshift bivouacs. He got away with it until March 1813, when they were reintroduced on a scale of three per company. The mules needed to carry these tents were released by the simultaneous introduction of individual mess tins to each soldier to replace the large communal camp kettles or 'Flanders cauldrons'.

Pay and rationing

Whenever possible, soldiers were still paid their daily subsistence money and left to their own devices as to how they fed themselves on home service. James Anton recorded that the soldiers were generally "perfectly contented" with this arrangement:

"We breakfasted about nine in the morning, on bread and milk; dined about two in the afternoon, on potatoes and a couple of salt herrings, boiled in the pot with the potatoes; a bottle of small-beer and a slice of bread served for supper, when we were disposed to take that meal, which soldiers seldom do. On the whole, I am certain our expenses for messing, dear as markets were, did not exceed three shillings and sixpence each, weekly."

On active service, rations were, as usual, issued in place of subsistence money, and in 1802 the soldier's official daily ration was one pound of bread (actually hard-tack biscuit) or one and a half pounds of flour, a pound of beef or half a pound of pork, and smaller quantities of peas, butter, cheese and rice, issued weekly. Providing all of this was actually issued to the soldier, it was sufficient to keep body and soul together, but hardly represented a balanced diet. Wherever possible, therefore, it was supplemented by local purchases, sometimes carried out at company or even battalion level, but more frequently by individual messes – eight to a dozen men who lived together in the same tent or barrack-room – or the soldiers' wives, who did most of the cooking. Ideally, local purchasing would be confined to any convenient markets, but when it became necessary to travel further afield, purchasing could all too easily turn into 'foraging' and possible entanglement with the army's disciplinary system.

Sir Ralph Abercrombie (1734-1801). Although his early career was not particularly distinguished, Abercrombie did well in the West Indies in the 1790s, emerged with some credit from the Helder debacle in 1799 and thoroughly restored the rather battered confidence of the army by his brilliantly successful campaign in Egypt.

Discipline and punishment

For any soldier found to be guilty of any military or civil crime a wide variety of punishments were available, ranging from death all the way down to extra guard duties. The choice of punishment was dictated by the severity of the offence. Normally only a general court martial could award the death penalty – for murder, desertion, or mutiny; as a lesser alternative, heavy floggings could be awarded, up to a maximum of 1,200 lashes. Soldiers could also be transferred to service in penal battalions such as the New South Wales Corps or the Royal African Corps, but were regularly offered such an alternative by way of commuting a death sentence. Civil prisoners turned over to the army also ended up in these units rather than regiments of the line.

Regimental court martials generally dealt with less serious offences, including some first-time deserters who at least had the common decency to run away from the enemy rather than deserting to them. Sentences from these courts tended to be expressed in lashes, although the men concerned, if reckoned to be incorrigible villains, could afterwards be turned over to penal battalions, or even occasionally to the Royal Navy. Offences dealt with at company level were more likely to result in the award of extra duties or other non-corporal punishments.

It should perhaps be stressed that surviving orderly books, such as those of the 25th Foot, show that responsibility for the maintenance of discipline rested in the first instance with the sergeants, and that in the majority of cases it was they rather than the officers who arrested and laid charges against offenders. In part, this simply reflects the fact that then, as now, they were in close everyday contact with the rank and file.

Soldiers pitching tents – a useful illustration of the old wedge-type tent, which was largely replaced by the bell-tent in the 1790s. (NMS)

CAREER PATTERNS

A striking feature of career patterns is the high turnover in personnel experienced by all units, irrespective of whether they were on active service or comfortably posted in garrisons. Out of 36 rank and file mustered in the ranks of the Grenadier Company of 1/Royals in October 1788, only 22 were still serving in the battalion by December 1793. Given that the battalion had been on Jamaica for all but four months of the intervening period, these losses are, if anything, rather on the low side. Out of 498 privates in the 68th Foot who sailed from Gibraltar to the West Indies in 1794, only 29 were still serving as privates when it returned home in 1797.

The turnover experienced by the 100th/92nd (Gordon) Highlanders was perhaps more typical, since after being raised in 1794 they spent the first few years of their existence in quiet Mediterranean garrisons, before being posted to Ireland in 1798 and subsequently taking part in the Helder expedition of 1799. Nevertheless, in 1794 alone, 13 men died of various causes, eight were transferred to other units, two were discharged and seven deserted. The following year was even worse, with 35 dead and 29 discharged, while 1796 saw 19 dead and 13 discharged. In 1797 six died, one was transferred, 13 were discharged and two deserted. On their return to Britain in 1798, the opportunity was taken to discharge no fewer than 44 men and transfer two to other units. Only four men died that year and one deserted, but in 1799 they were shot at for the first time and 86 men were killed, most of them at Bergen on 2 October. As for other losses, 23 men were discharged that year and a further 41 in 1800, largely as a result of wounds suffered at Bergen. In

View of Seringapatam 1794. Note the short jackets and varied headgear worn by the group on the left. (NMS)

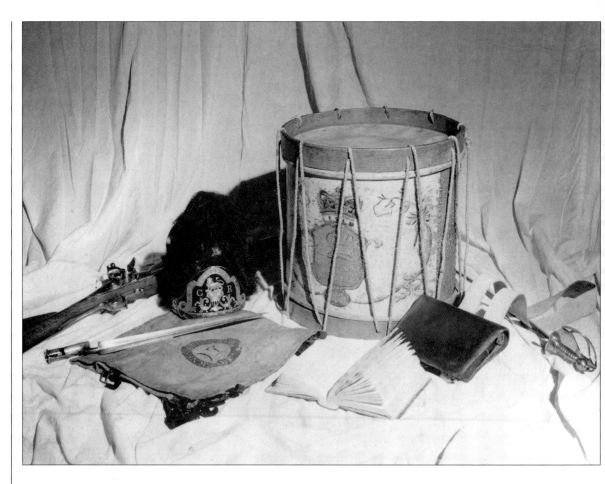

Drum and other equipment belonging to the 97th (Inverness-shire) Regiment, 1794-5. The knapsack, of the folding type, is yellow ochre in colour, with a green ring enclosing the regimental number. Note how thin the cartridge box is. (NMS)

addition eight men contrived to desert and for some reason five more were granted commissions.

Looking at turnover from a slightly different perspective, out of 471 private soldiers in the ranks of the 2/73rd Foot who fought at Waterloo in 1815, only 50 survived out of the original intake of 1809 (a handful had been promoted to non-commissioned rank). No fewer than 40% of the men had joined the battalion as recently as 1813, and a further 30% in 1812, so that only 30% of the privates had been serving in it for more than three years.

Service in the West Indies often distorted these figures quite dramatically, although once again it is important to view them in perspective. The greatest killer was undoubtedly mosquito-borne Yellow Fever, but although to some extent endemic, its effects tended to be felt as a series of epidemics, one of which unfortunately coincided with the campaign on San Domingo. Yellow Fever was survivable; indeed, having survived, a victim was 'salted' against further attacks. Unfortunately, all too many sufferers were already too debilitated by the Atlantic crossing – all 39 recruits for 1/Royals who came off the *Lively* in late 1794 were mustered as "convalescent" on their arrival – and were often finished off by liberal doses of raw rum smuggled into the hospitals by well-meaning comrades.

Despite having signed up for life, the majority of soldiers appear to have been discharged in their late thirties or early forties. Others were obviously discharged earlier, as a result of incapacitating wounds or other major injuries – frequently as long as a year after receiving them. The reasons most commonly cited for discharging an individual seem to have been rather less dramatic: rheumatism or, all too frequently, simply "worn out" (especially after service in the East or West Indies).

Promotion

There is no discernible pattern of promotion among non-commissioned ranks, and a surprising number were made up to sergeant within a year of joining their units – although in most, but by no means all, instances they were volunteers from the militia, sometimes with substantial service behind them. Basic literacy was naturally a prerequisite for all substantive promotions. Ordinarily, however, the fact that it was generally reckoned to take a year to train a soldier properly ensured that promotion to corporal and then to sergeant took correspondingly longer.

Throughout the period covered by this study, the only substantive ranks to which the ordinary soldier could aspire were corporal and sergeant. The titles of sergeant major, quartermaster sergeant, armourer sergeant, schoolmaster sergeant, pay sergeant and, from July 1813, colour sergeant were all appointments rather than ranks, although they did attract slightly more pay. A sergeant major, for example, would draw two shillings and three farthings daily, while an ordinary sergeant had to get by on one shilling and tenpence three farthings. Probably of rather more value were the traditional perks and opportunities which such appointments brought. To give but one example, a man named Paton, serving as armourer sergeant in the 42nd Highlanders, had a nice sideline in making officers' pistols.

As in the 18th century, it was possible for some to go further and attain commissioned rank. It has been estimated that about 10% of officers serving in the British army during the Napoleonic War had risen from the ranks – a figure broadly in line with the 18th century army.

In theory, the qualifications necessary to become an officer were remarkably simple: candidates had to be over 16, able to read and write, and be in possession of a recommendation from an officer of field rank – ie at least a major. There was also an upper age limit of 21, but this was only applied to new entrants and was invariably waived for men with previous service in the ranks. There was no other formal or social qualification, and out of five privates serving in the 100th (Gordon) Highlanders who were given commissions in 1799,

Private, 42nd Highlanders c1792, by Dayes. Although painted as a private, the inclusion of a broadsword, dirk and pistol would suggest a senior NCO. (NMS)

four were described at the time of their enlistment in 1794 as "labourers" and the fifth was a tailor.

As in the 18th century, promoted rankers generally fell into three categories: those who had earned their commission through some particular act of gallantry and those who had obtained it through sheer ability seem together to have accounted for just over half; the remainder was made up of the ever-present handful of volunteers who were serving in the ranks only until such time as they might be recommended for a vacant commission, either in their own or in some other corps.

There was no guarantee that, having been commissioned, a former ranker would remain with his original unit. Unless he was being promoted specifically in order to fill a vacancy which had arisen, he might be posted to another unit where a vacancy did exist. This happened quite frequently to men who were promoted solely as a reward for conspicuous bravery and who were otherwise unsuitable for service as a regimental officer. Such an appointment was obviously something of a dead end, although the recipient's standard of living might be higher and a reasonable pension assured. However, if a man was fit for it, his humble origins alone were no bar to further promotion.

Storming of Seringapatam. Note that although some officers are wearing round hats, the grenadiers still have their bearskins, and the Highlanders are in kilts and feathered bonnets. (NMS)

TRAINING AND TACTICS

Training, or learning his 'discipline', naturally occupied a good deal of a soldier's time. Recruits were intensively drilled, two or three times daily for about six or seven months, first in foot drill, then in manual exercise and finally platooning. After this they would be considered fit to take part in the normal training of the battalion.

In 1793 recruits joined their battalion immediately if it was stationed at home or in Ireland. If it was serving overseas they were posted to the recruit depot at Chatham and, in theory at least, would then be shipped out to join their relevant units after they had completed basic training. It was considered essential that the recruit be removed as far away as possible from his home, friends and any possible incentives or aids to tempt him to desert. The new regiments, so hastily raised in 1794, tended to exchange establishments at the earliest opportunity to counter any such desires. The first commissions in Bulwer's 106th (Norwich Rangers), for example, were signed in May 1794 and the regiment then embarked at Liverpool for Ireland on 8 November 1794. There they worked up their training for their first inspection the following summer. Units raised in Ireland, such as Vere Hunt's 135th Loyal Irish Volunteers, crossed to England in the same way. Naturally enough this practice ceased with the reduction of many of the new units, and the old system came back into use. If a man could join his unit immediately, he did so – which was easy if it had a second battalion; otherwise he received his basic training at one of the district recruiting headquarters that had been established by the Duke of York in 1795.

That year the Duke had also laid down a standard programme: Mondays and Fridays were to be devoted to battalion level drills; Thursdays and Saturdays to brigade drill; and Wednesdays to field days – 'exercises' in modern parlance. Sunday was of course the biblical day of rest, but Thursdays were also allowed to be a day off – although this was a privilege which could be withdrawn at any time if a battalion's 'discipline' was deemed to be below acceptable standards.

Although its actual bayonet strength could fluctuate quite wildly, an infantry battalion normally consisted of a small staff and ten companies, each theoretically comprising three commissioned officers, four sergeants, five corporals, two drummers and 95 privates.

One company was designated as grenadiers and the other as light infantry. Both of these 'flank' companies were to a certain extent independent of their parent battalion, and were frequently hived off with companies from other units to form provisional battalions, either of grenadiers or light infantry. It was not unknown to also find them as mixed 'flank battalions'. The Duke of Wellington made little if any use of such units, mostly because his armies were sufficiently large enough not to require them, but in other theatres of war throughout the period they were formed almost as a matter of course.

For operational purposes the eight remaining 'centre' or 'battalion' companies of the infantry battalion could be linked in pairs to form four 'grand divisions'. These were ordinarily used for nothing more than carrying out certain drill manoeuvres, but they occasionally formed the basis of distinct tactical units. (When 1/Royals were first posted to San Domingo, in 1794, the flank companies joined a provisional unit commanded by Major Brent Spencer of the 13th Foot, and the four grand divisions made up of the battalion companies were scattered in different garrisons.) In normal circumstances, however, the company was the basic tactical unit within the battalion; it could, if necessary, also be further broken down into two subdivisions.

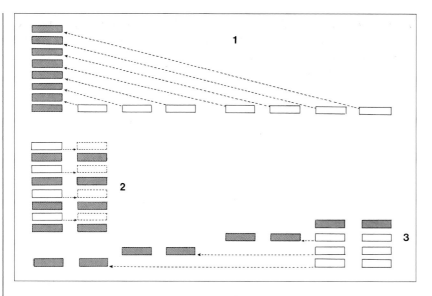

Dundas: Eighteen Manoeuvres. This sequence is based upon a slightly simplified version of the 1792 *Regulations*, published in 1794 by Sergeant Thomas Langley of the 1st Royal Regiment Tower Hamlets Militia. It assumes that a battalion is made up of only eight rather than ten companies, but although reference is made to grenadier and light infantry companies, the drill is actually that which would be practised by a battalion that had detached its flank companies to serve in provisional units – the normal practice in the British army at the time. It is also clear that in this version, companies are drawn up in the by now normal two ranks rather than the three demanded by Dundas. Throughout the sequence, the battalion is depicted facing the reader, (the battalion right is to the left of the diagram). 1. Close Column in Rear, Grenadiers. As with all of Dundas' manoeuvres this one actually contains three distinct elements. Firstly, the battalion forms column of companies behind the right flank company, assumed in this case to be the grenadiers. Secondly the even-numbered companies move out and forward in order to form a column of divisions (paired companies) and thirdly, the column of dividions redeploys into line.

DRILL BOOKS

General Sir Henry Bunbury famously remarked of the army in 1794: "Each colonel of a regiment managed it according to his own notions, or neglected it altogether. There was no uniformity of drill or movement; professional pride was rare; professional knowledge still more so."

This frequently repeated criticism was, broadly speaking, valid, but it does require some considerable qualification. 'Drill' and 'movement' (or 'manoeuvres') were two quite different things. The first, normally referred to as the 'manual' and 'platoon' exercises, was essentially basic foot drill and weapon handling, while the second was a fairly elaborate set of drills governing the tactical handling of battalions.

It is quite misleading to suggest that neither was standardised, for both were governed by official regulations and indeed had been regulated a century or more (see Warrior 19). The difficulty in 1794 lay not in any want of official regulations but rather in enforcing those which did exist. In part this was due to the individual notions of commanding officers and the unofficially tolerated 'traditional' drill movements practised by some regiments, but it also reflected the confusion arising from the haste with which the army had been expanded.

The army had gone into the American War using the 1764 *Regulations*, and in 1778 a new updated set was introduced, in line with the latest tactical thinking. Unfortunately, the fact that there happened to be a major war on at the time not only hampered the introduction of the 1778 *Regulations*, but effectively killed them off. Moreover, the widespread adoption of light infantry style tactics in America introduced yet another complicating factor, so that for much of the decade following the War some regiments were regularly reported to be faithfully following the 1764 *Regulations*, and others were quite properly conducting themselves according to the newer, 1778, *Regulations*; still others were either supplementing them both with 'traditional' manoeuvres of their own devising or even ignoring them completely.

There was in effect a very real gulf between those regiments that had been stationed in Britain or Ireland and there had assiduously learned the theoretical aspects of their profession, at the expense of practical experience, and those regiments that had served in North America and gained a wealth of practical experience, often quite at odds with the theory being promoted by the military hierarchy.

Dundas's 1792 Regulations

It was against this highly unsatisfactory background that Colonel David Dundas published his *Principles of Military Movements* in 1788. Humphrey Bland's privately published *Treatise of Military Discipline* had dominated British tactical doctrines and formed the basis for the official drill regulations for much of the 18th century, and Dundas' book did the same thing 60 years later. At the time Dundas was serving on the Irish staff, and for once in its miserable existence, the Irish army managed to take the lead in introducing an excellent programme of reform. Between 1789 and 1791 all the regiments serving in Ireland were trained according to Dundas' principles, and in the following year a condensed edition of his book became the 1792 *Regulations*.

Under normal circumstances regiments that had not been part of the Irish establishment could not have expected to become fully proficient in the new drills until the following summer, particularly since so many of them were dispersed in overseas garrisons. After February of 1793, however, circumstances were anything but normal. As in 1778, not only did the old regiments once again have more important things to worry about than assimilating new drill books in the middle of a major war, but the new regiments were also placed at even more of a disadvantage.

The officers who joined the new regiments fell broadly into three categories. First there were those who were joining the army for the first time and who were just as ignorant of the drill book as the recruits they were expected to lead. Secondly, in order to ensure at least a leavening of experience, a large proportion of the officers were taken from the half-pay list. Some – perhaps most – had been idle since the close of the American War ten years earlier, and if they had not forgotten their drill,

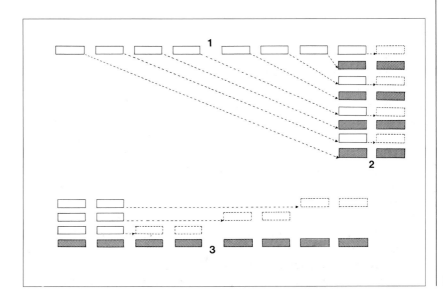

Dundas 2. **Close Column in Front of Light Infantry. Essentially this manoeuvre is a mirror-image of No.1, in which a column of companies is formed in front of the left flank company.**

the 1764 one they remembered had now been superseded, and their knowledge therefore of little relevance.

The third group was made up of serving officers who had transferred from old regiments to new ones in order to gain at least one step in rank. Once they actually succeeded in joining their new units, their services may have been much appreciated, but all too often there was, for various reasons, an appreciable time lag between their leaving one regiment and joining another – particularly if their original unit was serving overseas at the time of their appointment. As a result, and because of the necessary detachment of some officers on recruiting, the new regiments, through no real fault of their own, were desperately short both of experience and of officers on the ground.

When William Earle Bulwer's 106th (Norwich Rangers) were inspected at New Geneva on 13 June 1795, they were reported to be well clothed and mustering 932 rank and file, 82 NCOs and 22 drums. By any standards this was respectable, but besides those recruiting, seven of the officers were absent, and the regiment's drill was so bad that the inspecting general refused to pass them fit for service until they had completely satisfied him at a repeat inspection on 4 August. Ironically, no sooner had they been pronounced efficient than the regiment was reduced, at Spike Island, and its men drafted into other corps.

Excellent though the 1792 *Regulations* were, they could quite easily have followed the 1778 *Regulations* into virtual oblivion. Once again it was the Duke of York who took the matter firmly in hand. After his appointment as commander-in-chief, in 1795, he insisted on enforcing strict compliance with the 1792 *Regulations*, and thereafter was very vigilant in detecting and dealing with any deviations.

Like his great predecessor, Humphrey Bland, David Dundas had the

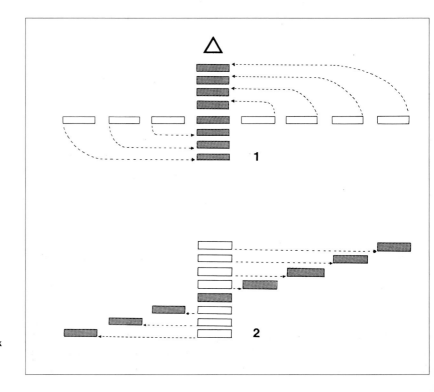

Dundas: 3. **Close Column on a Central Company, Facing to the Rear. In the first exercise the companies file out and round to form a column of companies facing to the rear. Having done so they then counter-march on the spot – i.e. the front and rear ranks face to the right and left respectively and file around briskly to change places, thus bringing the front rank men back into the true front, after which the battalion redeploys into line.**

3rd or Scots Regiment of
Footguards, St James's Palace
c. 1790. (NMS)

rare ability to express himself clearly and elegantly. In the circumstances this was just as well, for the great virtue of his drill book was that it provided a battalion with a standardised repertoire of simple manoeuvres which could be applied to any tactical situation.

Although Dundas readily acknowledged the influence of the Prussian von Saldern, his *Principles* were by no means an adaptation of Prussian drill, but rather a logically set out system, deeply rooted in existing tactical doctrine.

New firing system

Throughout the greater part of the 18th century the British army's officers had been concerned, above all, with winning the firefight, and they had strived to improve their platoon firing systems as a way of achieving this. In North America the practice had grown up of fighting in open order, but Dundas rejected this in favour of the more traditional close order:

"The company is formed three deep. The files lightly touch when firelocks are shouldered, but without crowding – each man will occupy about 22 inches...

"Close order is the chief and primary order when the battalion and its parts assemble and form – open order is only regarded as an exception and occasionally used in situations of parade and show. In close order the officers are in the ranks, and the rear ranks are closed up one pace. In open order the officers are advanced three paces, and the ranks are two paces distant from each other."

Although Dundas (and the Duke of York) was successful in suppressing the "loose files and American scramble" championed by veterans of the American War, the two-deep line had come to stay, and three ranks only occasionally surfaced on the parade ground in order to satisfy unusually punctilious inspecting officers.

The manual exercise included in the 1792 *Regulations* was very similar to those praticed in 1764, and the alterations that were introduced appear to have been necessitated by the insistence on closing up the frontage to 22 inches per man. For example, where the 1764 manual exercise directed the soldier to carry his firelock across the body when priming it, the 1792 version required him to level it waist high, muzzle towards the enemy.

Almost as a matter of course the new manual also included an improved method of locking the ranks for firing. While a soldier quite literally needed a reasonable amount of elbow-room in order to load his firelock, it was universally agreed that having done so he and the rest of the men in his file should then close up or 'lock' as tightly as possible before firing. Dundas, as we have seen, laid down that in close order there should only be a single pace between each rank. In order to lock, the front rank knelt down, as in previous drills, and the second rank closed up, now so tightly that their knees were pressed into the backs of the front rank men, while the left shoulder of the man in the third rank was pressed into the right shoulder-blade of the centre rank man. Unfortunately this meant that the men in the centre rank had to stand pretty well square on to their front when firing, but in practice when battalions fought in two ranks instead of the prescribed three, it was the front rank which was abandoned. The two remaining ranks both fired standing (there is no evidence for one rank kneeling and only the second standing) and without the kneeling first rank to get in the way, both were able to adopt a more natural stance.

The platoon exercise was also little more than an updated version of that authorised in 1764. Companies (with the exception of the two flank companies) were to be "equalised in point of numbers", in order to function as platoons. Platoons could then fire in sequence from right to left, from the centre to the flanks and vice versa, in grand divisions, in wings – two grand divisions – and even by the whole battalion at once. In all cases, fire control was normally exercised by specifying the number of rounds to be fired.

It used to be thought that the acknowledged superiority of the British infantry in the Peninsula was due to their ability to pour sus-

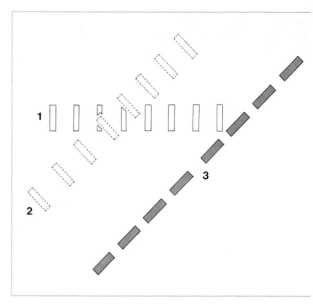

Dundas 4. **Change of Position in Open Column.** The battalion moving from left to right in open column of companies is first ordered to change direction, which it does by means of each company wheeling backwards into the new alignment. The column is then temporarily halted to allow it to reform properly, after which it may then wheel into line by companies

Dundas 5. **Wings Thrown Back.** A relatively straightforward manoeuvre, in which the companies first wheel backwards and then, facing about, march forward into the new position.

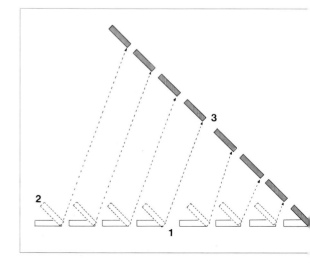

Private, flank company 79th
Highlanders, with family in Paris
1815. (NMS)

tained fire into the enemy. Yet the striking feature of British infantry tactics throughout the Revolutionary and Napoleonic Wars is how few rounds were actually fired in combat. Up to the outbreak of the American War, British officers had been passionately interested, to the point of obsession, in ways of improving the platoon firing. However, experience in North America had shown that casualties could be minimised by advancing straight on the objective, firing only one or perhaps two volleys at the most and then going in with the bayonet. In the short term this might involve casualties, while closing up on the objective, but in the longer term it achieved that objective with fewer casualties and without the disorganisation engendered by a prolonged firefight.

While platoon firing certainly remained an important element of

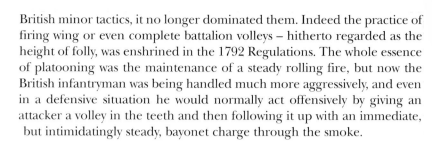

British minor tactics, it no longer dominated them. Indeed the practice of firing wing or even complete battalion volleys – hitherto regarded as the height of folly, was enshrined in the 1792 Regulations. The whole essence of platooning was the maintenance of a steady rolling fire, but now the British infantryman was being handled much more aggressively, and even in a defensive situation he would normally act offensively by giving an attacker a volley in the teeth and then following it up with an immediate, but intimidatingly steady, bayonet charge through the smoke.

The 'eighteen manoeuvres'

The core of Dundas' work was, of course, his celebrated *Eighteen Manoeuvres*. The ever ascerbic Bunbury had scarcely drawn breath from deploring the lack of a standardised drill when he went on to mock that Dundas "made the fatal mistake of distributing the whole science of war into eighteen manoeuvres which were a sad stumbling block to dull-witted officers". In point of fact, this criticism fails on two grounds. Tactical systems should, in the first place, always be kept as simple as possible, but in any case there were actually more than just 18 manoeuvres in Dundas' system, since most of them incorporated two or more quite distinct evolutions. The *Eighteen Manoeuvres*, far from being a rigidly limited repertoire, were in fact a standard programme of exercises to be demonstrated before an inspecting officer. Such inspections were no empty formality and by enforcing this standardised testing system, a general could satisfy himself that the drill regulations were being properly complied with , that the battalion was capable of competently undertaking every prescribed manoeuvre and, ultimately, whether it was fit for active service.

It was perhaps unhelpful that the condensed version of Dundas' book, appearing as the 1792 *Regulations*, omitted many of his original notes describing when and under what tactical circumstances a particular manoeuvre should be attempted. The purpose of some, perhaps most, of them is clear enough; the immediate value of others is less obvious. Certainly some permitting minor alterations of a battalion's position appear rather over-complicated, but it must be borne in mind that a very great deal of training has confidence-building as its ultimate aim. A battalion which could carry out complicated manoeuvres swiftly, competently and with utter confidence on a parade ground would obviously be well equipped amidst the chaos of the battlefield. Indeed, the success of the aggressive tactical handling of British infantry characteristic of this period was entirely dependent on this confident competence or "discipline".

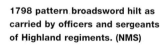

1798 pattern broadsword hilt as carried by officers and sergeants of Highland regiments. (NMS)

Evolution of light infantry tactics

Another, and perhaps more valid, criticism of Dundas' work is the apparent lack of attention paid to light infantry tactics. Yet again this criticism is misconceived. Dundas certainly argued of light infantry that "instead of being considered an accessory to the battalion, they have become the principal feature of our army [in 1788] and have almost put grenadiers out of fashion". Light infantry, he admitted elsewhere, had their uses, but his own speciality was "heavy" infantry, and his drill book is concerned with manoeuvring and fighting a battalion of the line.

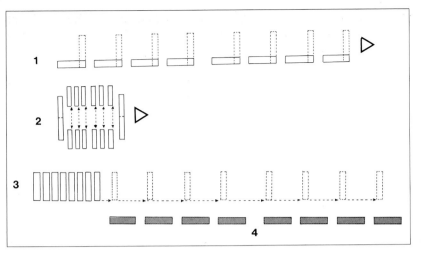

Dundas 6. Counter-march and Change of Position. First the battalion forms an open column of companies by wheeling each one backwards to the left and then countermarching to bring the front rank men back into the front. Secondly, having closed up, the battalion forms a solid square: "At the words, Outwards face, all the Companies face from their Center, the Right Subdivisions to the Right, and the Left to the Left, except the Front and Rear (Sub)Divisions, those two Divisions face into the Center; at the word, March, they file into the Square from the center of the two companies... The Square is reduced in like manner..." Having successfully completed that exercise to the inspecting officer's satisfaction, the battalion once again formed an open column of companies from the rear. The first (rear) company stood fast, while the second was halted by the first captain once it reached the required distance; the third was then halted by the second captain and so on. Having thus formed the column, the companies counter-march and then wheel back into line.

Each battalion had a company of light infantry as "an accessory", and the ten pages devoted to their employment in the 1792 *Regulations* are entirely adequate to cover their limited role within the battalion.

Notwithstanding Dundas' views on the matter, the average battalion's organic light infantry element actually increased during the period. In addition to the light infantry company, the grenadiers were usually also trained to act as skirmishers, and even, it would seem, the battalion companies too in some units. In addition, those men belonging to the battalion companies who could shoot straight were also designated as skirmishers, and were variously referred to as "marksmen" or "flankers". Normally they remained with their companies, but so well established was this practice that in 1806 Sir John Stuart not only formed the flank companies of the battalions under his command into provisional battalions, but culled the flankers as well to reinforce the light infantry battalion.

Viewed simply in terms of numbers, the British army was well enough

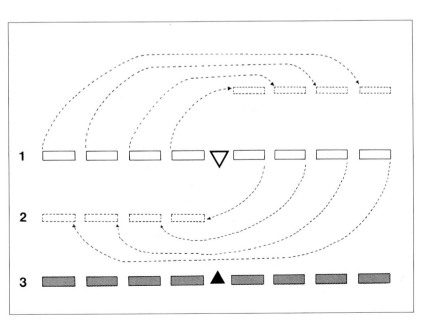

Dundas 7. Counter-march by Files on the Centre of the Regiment. A relatively straightforward manoeuvre in which the battalion reverses its position by counter-marching. The movement is greatly exaggerated here for the sake of clarity – each company having faced in to the centre needed to take only three paces to the right (or two if in two ranks) before countermarching and moving into position.

Surrender of Seringapatam –
once again note that while the
officers and gunners wear round
hats, the grenadiers are still
wearing bearskin caps. (NMS)

provided with light infantry in the 1790s, but the weakness lay in its tactical doctrines – or rather the conspicuous lack of them. The 1792 Regulations only covered the employment of regimental light infantry companies, which was all very well if that company remained close to its parent battalion or else was employed independently on some appropriate service. The problem was that commanders in the field tended to require the services of more than one company, and so almost invariably formed all those available into a provisional battalion. However, there were no formal drills covering the employment of battalion-sized groups of light infantry, so the drills and training remained largely company orientated – although the individual battalions must have worked out their own solutions.

The real need was to balance the requirement for dedicated light infantry units with the equally pressing need for ordinary infantry battalions to retain a skirmisher element within their ranks. The solution therefore was to convert regiments of the line into light infantry regiments, allowing the light companies to remain with their parent battalions. This somewhat draconian policy was not quite as radical as it is sometimes represented, however, for the skirmishing role of these units was quite limited.

The first two units to be retrained, the 43rd and 52nd Regiments of Foot and the 95th Rifles, were formed into the famous Light Division, while the 51st and 68th, together with a number of foreign units, formed the 7th Division, which always regarded itself as a light division. Although both divisions were clearly capable of skirmishing, their actual deployment tended to be in the 18th century tradition, and their light infantry role was more strategic than tactical – undertaking raids, fast marches, forming security cordons and so on.

On the battlefield the light infantry role was assumed first and foremost by the battalion light infantry companies, supplemented, in the Peninsula at least, by a company of riflemen and, more often than not, by ordinary battalion company soldiers (see **Plate J**).

The tactical employment of skirmishers was relatively straight-forward. It normally involved the use of loose open formations based either on pairs of infantrymen (although for the widest dispersion they were grouped in fours). Light infantrymen were also expected to be able to think for themselves, take advantage of whatever cover offered itself and, above all, to take proper aim at the enemy. A considerably increased allocation of ball ammunition was issued both to light infantry and to rifle units in training, although it should be stressed that in neither case were recruits selected for any skill which they displayed in that field.

The rifle was far more accurate than the common firelock, and there are numerous examples recorded of excellent shooting, both on ranges and in the field. However, possession of a good weapon will not turn a poor shot into a marksman. Even today it is remarkable how many soldiers have difficulty in hitting a man-sized target at 300 metres. There is no doubt that there were some excellent marksmen in the ranks of the 60th and 95th Rifles and in other regiments as well, but then, as now, they were the exception, and in more modern times would be the mainstay of the battalion shooting team. Moreover, standards of marks-manship have a tendency to fall off dramatically when the target is shooting back; this might explain why no real attempt was made to interlock fields of fire. In theory it should have been possible to post riflemen behind light infantry to allow them to snipe at useful targets without the fear of being overrun by a determined bayonet attack. In practice, however, riflemen were invariably posted out beyond the light infantry and then retired behind them when threatened.

THE PLATES

A: VOLUNTEERING FROM THE MILITIA.

Although the traditional form of recruiting by beat of drum was practised throughout the period covered by this study, considerable numbers of militiamen were permitted and indeed encouraged to volunteer for service in the line. Ordinarily the Militia laws specifically forbade this practice and special Acts of Parliament were necessary to authorise it between specific dates. At first this was resorted to only infrequently, the first such Acts being passed in 1798 and 1799, but from 1805 the practice became more frequent and developed into an annual process from 1807.

The 1807 Act allowed for up to 40 per cent of a particular Militia battalion's actual strength to volunteer for service in the regulars after receiving an order for that purpose – generally in April or May for Scottish and English units. This order would also specify which units the men could volunteer into, normally either newly established second battalions or those older battalions which required rebuilding after prolonged service overseas.

Once five sixths of the authorised number had been accepted they were to be turned over to their new units within 30 days. However if less than five sixths of the quota had volunteered within that period, the commanding officer was required to parade his battalion again and 'explain' the terms of enlistment, after which a further ten days would be allowed for recruiting. If the quota still remained unfulfilled a third and final attempt could be made three months later. In such cases according to a private named James Moore, who transferred from the King's Own Staffordshire Militia to the 2nd Battalion 73rd Foot on the 12th May 1812, a considerable amount of pressure was sometimes exerted on the would-be recruits:

"The Militia would be drawn up in line, and the officers, or non-commissioned officers, from the Regiments requiring volunteers, would give a glowing description of their several Regiments, describing the victories they had gained and the honours they had acquired, and conclude by offering, as a bounty, to volunteers for life £14; to volunteers for the limited period of seven years, £11. If these inducements were not effectual in getting men, then coercive measures were adopted; heavy and long drills, and field exercises were forced on them; which were so oppressive, that to escape them, the men would embrace the alternative and join the regulars."

There was clearly a problem in finding volunteers from the Staffordshire Militia that year, but none of the other recruits from the Militia who left an account of the process mentions these measures being necessary.

Private William Wheeler of the 2nd Royal Surrey Militia simply says that in 1809 he:

"volunteered together with 127 of my comrades into the 51st Light Infantry Regiment. I had made up my mind to volunteer but into what regiment I cared not a straw, so I determined to go with the greatest number. The latter end of March the order came. On the 1st. April I gave my name in for the 51st. Upwards of 90 men volunteered in to the 95th Rifle Regiment. I was near going to this Regt. myself for it was always a fancy

Regimental pattern broadsword hilt carried by Breadalbane Fencibles and 116th Highlanders. (NMS)

Corps of mine, and another cause was that Lieut Foster a good officer beloved by every man in the Corps I had left, volunteered into the 95th. But I had made up my mind to go with the strongest party."

Three years later James Anton, a 24-year old weaver from Huntly, serving in the Aberdeenshire Militia was similarly undiscriminating as to his choice of regiment:

"My friend Huntly had been promoted some time previously to be a corporal, and perhaps with this small step of promotion his ambition soared; and as little prospect of further advancement appeared to gratify his views (they were then guarding French prisoners-of-war near Dalkeith), he determined to volunteer his service to the Line. His remark was, 'I serve at present secure of life and limb, but with no prospect of future benefit in old age, which I may attain; it is better to hazard both abroad in the regular service, than have poverty and hard labour accompanying me to a peaceful grave at home. 'I concurred in his opinion, and he forthwith waited on the commanding officer and signified his intention to volunteer into any regiment which that officer might be pleased to recommend. The offer was accepted in the most favourable manner, consequently my friend placed his name on the list for the 42nd (the regiment recommended), and

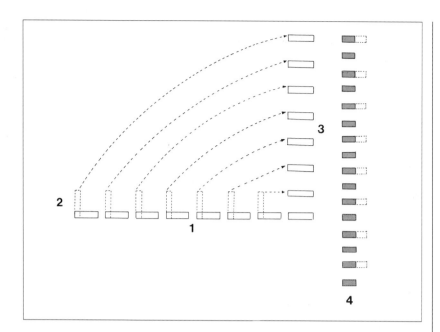

Dundas 8. **March in Open Column. All but the left flank company wheel backwards then form an open column of companies, after which the left hand subdivisions dress in front of the right hand subdivisions to form a close company of subdivisions.**

BELOW **Three-pint canteen marked up to No.2/ 68th (Durham) Light Infantry. Note the absence of the painted broad-arrow mark so often seen in reconstructions. This actually appears to have been branded on the "inside" face. (Author)**

Drummer, 100th (Gordon) Highlanders c1794. (NMS)

ABOVE **Magazine-tin covered with leather. Issued early in the period to supplement the ammunition carried in cartridge boxes, this was latterly abandoned in favour of a larger cartridge box. Although in theory a more sensible arrangement this meant that the soldier was carrying at least five pounds of lead on his right hip. (Queen's Own Highlanders)**

was not the last to follow the example; several others added their names to the roll, and after a few weeks, we were despatched to join the depot of the regiment at Inverness."

Anton did well for himself in the 42nd (Black Watch). He had initially enrolled, under-age, in the Aberdeenshire Militia in the winter of 1802, so that subsequently when he was attested at Dalkeith on the 6th of May 1812, he already had nine years service under his belt. It is hardly surprising therefore that he was quickly promoted to Sergeant little more than a month later, on the 12th of June – striking testimony as to the quality of recruits obtained from the Militia. He went on to serve in the Peninsular War and at Waterloo, and was appointed Quartermaster Sergeant on the 29th of June 1830, before being discharged with chronic rheumatism on the 30th of April 1833, having successfully secured the pension which tempted him to enlist in the first place.

It is difficult to overstate the crucial importance of volunteering from the Militia after 1805 and a surprising number of both the newly authorised Second battalions, and some older units as well were in fact predominantly made up of ex-militiamen. The enlisted men of the 2/73rd afford a striking example of this. During the Waterloo campaign in 1815 no fewer than 32 out of the 38 sergeants had volunteered from the Militia, together with 24 out of 29 Corporals. As for the rank and file; 299 are definitely identified as militiamen, while another 50 also appear from their dates of enlistment and other circumstances to have come from the Militia, making a total of 349 out of 471 rank and file. Former militiamen were only in a minority amongst the drummers, simply because they were normally recruited as boys and therefore had no place in the Militia to begin with.

Volunteering from the Militia

Private, 13th (1st Somersetshire) Regiment, San Domingo 1794 (See text commentary for detailed captions)

B

C

Light Infantry Training

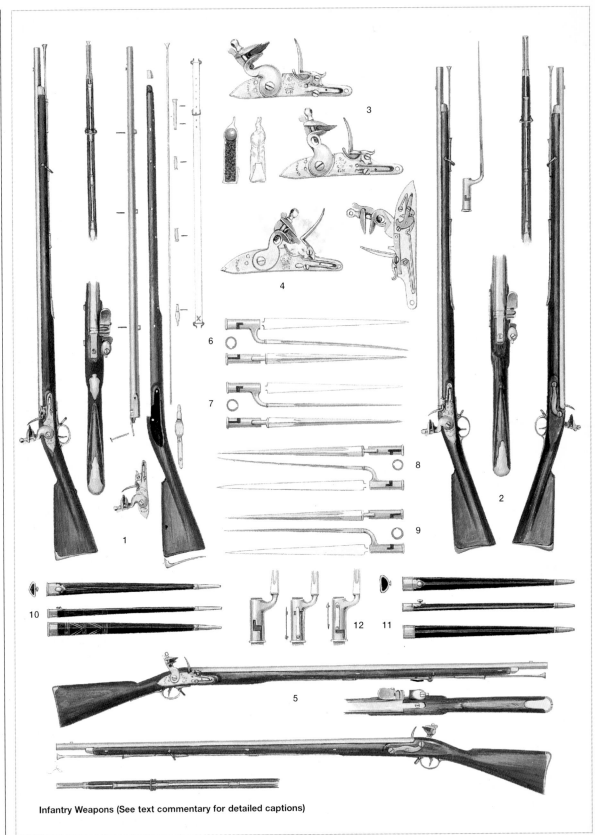

Infantry Weapons (See text commentary for detailed captions)

D

Halt on the March

Barrack Room Life

Line Infantry, Royal Scots, c. 1800s (See text commentary for detailed captions)

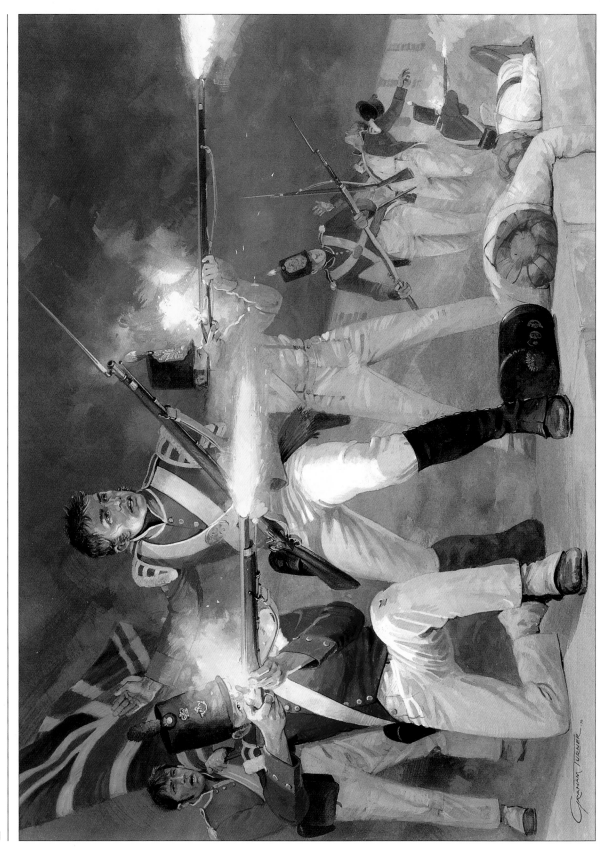

H

69th Foot at Velore, 1806

2a

2

3b

3a

1

5

5b

5a

4

Footwear (See text commentary for detailed captions)

J

79th Highlanders at Waterloo

Pioneer 21st Foot, 1815 (See text commentary for detailed captions)

K

After the Wars

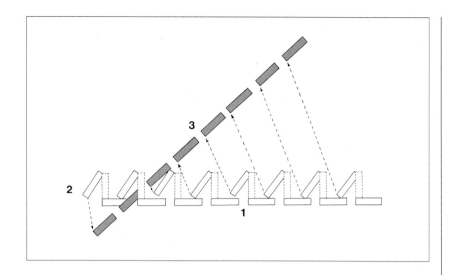

Dundas 9. **Echelon Change of Position. Not quite as complicated as it first appears, this manoeuvre allows a battalion to change position within a confined space – often an important consideration on actual service.**

B: PRIVATE, 13TH (1ST SOMERSETSHIRE) REGIMENT, SAN DOMINGO 1794

The outbreak of war with France in 1793 found a substantial number of regular units serving in the West Indies. One of them was the 13th Foot, which was sent from Jamaica to San Domingo (modern Haiti) in September 1793.

The population of the French colony was an unstable mixture of white planters, 'poor whites', mulattos and Negroes - most of the latter being slaves. The political turmoil fostered by the revolution in France quickly led to bloody anarchy in San Domingo and in desperation the white planters sought British intervention.

Two battalions, the 13th and the 49th, under Lieutenant Colonel John Whitelocke of the 13th landed at Jeremie on the 20th of September, without opposition and two days later the strategically important fortress of Mole St.Nicholas was also handed over by its pro-Royalist governor, Colonel Deneux. Some minor successes and failures followed, but it soon became obvious that Colonel Whitelocke lacked sufficient men with which to consolidate his rather precarious

position, let alone to go on to the offensive since his two battalions mustered only 677 men between them.

An unsuccessful action at Cape Tiburon on the 3rd February 1794 cost the 13th Foot two privates killed and another three wounded, besides Captain Charles Colville slightly wounded in the leg and Lieutenant George Dana of the Light Company wounded in the head. Further reinforcements were gradually dribbled in to Whitelocke virtually company by company, but it was not until the arrival of the flank companies of 1/Royals and the 20th Foot, later in the month, that any real military operations could be undertaken. As the ordinary battalion companies would be required for garrison duties, a provisional battalion was formed from the various flank companies under the command of Major Brent Spencer of the 13th.

This provisional unit immediately distinguished itself in the storming of a rebel-held fort at L'Acul on the 19th of February in which the 13th lost one man killed, together with a sergeant and another man wounded. All three men probably belonged to the Light Company. The Flank

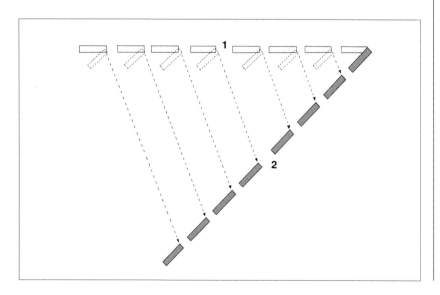

Dundas 10. **A New Line taken up by the Echelon Movement. A straightforward manoeuvre requiring no explanation.**

RIGHT **Platoon Exercise 9: Return Ramrods.** Note how the two ranks are carrying out the loading procedure at the one pace distance laid down in 1792.

OPPOSITE **Platoon Exercise: Present – Fire!** The kneeling third rank is dispensed with and both ranks lock in a more natural firing position. It is important, however, that the front rank crouches slightly; otherwise it is difficult for the second rank to avoid firing high. (Author)

Battalion was then shipped across to the Mole St.Nicholas and the four grenadier companies at took part in an abortive attack on a rebel-held post at Bombarde, some twelve miles away, in the early hours of the morning of the 1st May. The attack failed quite ignominiously although the 13th's Grenadier Company was lucky to escape with only three men – Private Andrew Gillaspy, Private James Merrit and Private William Rice – returned as killed. No further casualties were reported when the Flank Battalion subsequently took part in General Whyte's successful capture of the colony's capital, Port au Prince but thereafter all the regular units were very much on the defensive.

On the 19th of April 1794 district returns show that the 13th Foot had 5 sergeants, 4 drummers and 101 rank and file stationed at the Mole, (presumably belonging to the flank companies which were kept up to strength at the expense of the rest of the battalion) but only 3 sergeants, 3 drummers and 56 men were actually fit for duty. A detachment of the 13th at Leogane comprising 2 sergeants and 24 men could only muster a single sergeant and 6 men fit for duty. Another detachment at L'Arcahaye was rather healthier with only two men sick out of 36, while a fourth detachment at Tiburon was

perhaps more typical with 15 men sick out of 64. Such wide dispersion of sub-units was typical of service on San Domingo and it was in fact rare, in the early days, to find all of a battalion's companies serving together in one place.

Throughout the 18th century colonial warfare in the Caribbean had very largely been confined to the capture of the coastal towns. Once the ports were secured little resistance was expected, or experienced, in the hinterland. The threat came from a sea-borne counter-attack aimed at regaining control of the ports. Consequently the British army saw its first priority as defending those ports against a possible landing by French regulars. In the event this never came, but in the meantime a considerable number of colonial units were raised, or at least sponsored, to fight the 'Brigands' in the hills while the regulars were condemned to garrison duty in the unhealthy coastal strip. Opinion is divided as to whether the resultant mortality was primarily due to Yellow Fever or even to the chronic alcoholism engendered by the boredom of garrison life - though the strong belief by soldiers that rum was an effective medicine can hardly have helped.

At any rate, by August 1795 the 13th was down to just

60 men fit for duty and the survivors ordered home to recruit the regiment afresh.

1 This soldier wears the surprisingly comfortable uniform authorised for troops serving in the West Indies from 1790 onwards. It comprises a short red wool jacket - probably unlined – with collar, cuffs and shoulder straps in the regimental facing colour; in this case yellow. A contemporary sketch of operations on Martinique useful includes a number of rear views of British soldiers wearing this uniform, confirming that the jacket was a simple round garment without tails as had been worn during the American War. It was very much an undress article of clothing for wear on active service (developing into the equally popular shell-jacket) and as such it lacked the regimental lace which normally decorated the full-sized coat. The white linen trousers were also extremely practical, being much looser and more comfortable than the normal combination of tight woollen breeches, stockings and gaiters.

This particular individual is depicted in full marching order, which comprised **2** a folding canvas knapsack for spare clothing, **3** interior of cartridge box showing how it was attached to the white-buff cross belts, Just how this equipment was actually worn probably depended to some extent on regimental standing orders, but practical experience suggests that while the crossbelts and haversack sling should be secured under the shoulder-straps, the knapsack slings and canteen sling should lie *over* them. Given the nature of the operations undertaken by the 13th on San Domingo it is unlikely that the knapsack was in fact carried very often. **4** horse-hair stock and brass buckle, **5** cartridge and former **6** wooden two-quart water canteen, **7** linen haversack carrying rations and regulation issue tin mug, **8** the brush and picker, used for elementary cleaning of the gun lock were normally attached to one of the cross-belts and would have been particularly useful for clearing damp powder out of the priming pan. **9** a brass fife-case, **10** Lock cover, and **11** the wooden tompion, would have protected the contents of the barrel from tropical rain-storms.**12** Regimental button.

C: LIGHT INFANTRY TRAINING

Conversion of the 43rd and 52nd Regiments of Foot into light infantry units in 1803 was apparently hampered by the difficulty of retraining veteran officers and soldiers in the new

Piper Clarke and the 71st Highlanders at Vimeiro. An unusually accurate depiction of the fight by Atkinson. (NMS)

skills now demanded of them. Consequently it was decided that in future only 'young' regiments would be selected for conversion. Consequently, the newly raised 2/78th Highlanders were next chosen, but their training had to be cut short when they were ordered to Gibraltar. Then, following the outbreak of the Peninsular War in 1808, the 68th and the 85th Foot, were advised that they had been selected for light infantry training.

The 68th (Durham) at least was actually quite an old regiment, having originally been raised in 1756 as the 2/23rd, but recent service in the West Indies had reduced it to a mere 90 rank and file by 1806. Between September 1806 and June 1809 the regiment took on 925 recruits including 521 volunteers from the militia. Although the latter were obviously already trained in the ordinary close-order drill, their willingness to volunteer in the first place and indeed the atmosphere of a new unit made them much more amenable

to retraining than the old salts of the 43rd and 52nd who had been soldiers since God was a boy.

Baron Francis Rottenberg, who was in charge of light infantry training at Brabourne Lees was consequently able to report favourably on the 68th in May 1809. He also specifically commented on the fact that the new volunteers were: "particularly good and more adapted to the light service than the old men of the battalion." He was also very complimentary about their shooting – ball ammunition for target practice being issued on the same scale as to rifle regiments – but regretted the absence of too many officers recruiting and the fact that the battalion: "had not yet attained in its field exercise and movements when acting as troops of the line any great deal of precision, its whole time having been taken up with light infantry movements."

The plate depicts a typical moment in such light infantry training. Two soldiers, a Corporal and another experienced man are demonstrating the art of skirmishing according to the direction of an immaculately turned out Sergeant. The Corporal is taking aim at a hypothetical target, while covered by his rear rank man. Once the Corporal has fired his partner

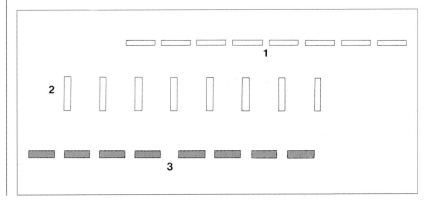

Dundas 11. Change of Position. Companies face to the right then wheel by files into open column of companies. Having reached the new position, they then wheel by companies back into line.

Corporal and Bandsman (in white jacket), 79th Highlanders 1815. (NMS)   **49**

will move up to six paces in front of him while he reloads. Although the rear rank man may then select a target, he is not to fire (except in an emergency of course), until the Corporal calls out READY! to signify that he has reloaded. At that point he may then open fire, whereupon the Corporal will move up to six paces beyond him and cover while he in turn reloads. Exactly the same procedure is followed in retreating except that once a man has fired he is permitted to fall back up to twelve paces behind the man covering him.

The conversion to light infantry status involved comparatively little alteration in the uniform and equipment. Regiments so designated continued to wear red jackets and were really only distinguished by the wearing of wings on the shoulders - a distinction hitherto confined to flank companies - and by the use of other traditional light infantry badges such as the bugle-horn on the front of the shako, and a green plume. The 68th had been wearing green facings

ever since 1758, but they were regarded as highly appropriate for a light infantry unit. In May 1821 Sergeant Wheeler of the 51st wrote: "we are in future to bear the title of 'The King's Own light infantry Regiment' and that the facings are to be changed from green to blue. We are of course all proud of the distinguished honor, I am afraid it will spoil the appearance of the Regiment. Green facings suits a Light Infantry Regiment..."

Crossbelts were slightly broader than normal, those ordered for the 52nd in 1805 being two and five-eighths of an inch broad in place of the two and one eighth inches specified in the 1802 regulations. On conversion to light infantry in 1808, the 68th and 85th were ordered to be "assimilated with regard to their clothing, arming and discipline to the 43rd and 52nd Regiments" so it may reasonably be supposed that they too received the broader belts as well as the new sixty-round ammunition pouch.

Dundas 12. **Retreat in Line.** A straightforward manoeuvre in which the whole battalion faces about, retreats a short distance, faces front to fire by companies, and then retires by alternate companies.

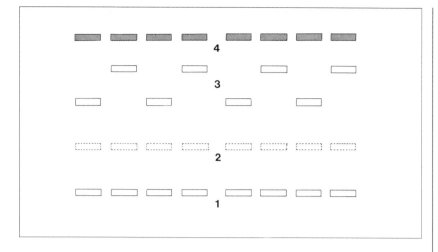

Eventually the 68th, in common with other light infantry units would be equipped with the New Land Pattern firelock. A light infantry version was approved as early as 1803 but not put into production until late 1811. For some years after their conversion therefore the 68th must have continued to carry the ordinary India Pattern firelock, though they may have browned the previously 'bright' barrels in best light infantry style. It is not known when the practice of parading with loosened slings became general.

D: INFANTRY WEAPONS

1 Short Land Pattern firelock: First set up for Dragoons in the 1740s, the Short Land Pattern officially superseded the Long Land Pattern in 1768 and by 1793 was the British army's standard infantry weapon. Production ceased in 1797 but the available evidence indicates that it continued to be used by low-numbered regular units into the early 1800s, and for considerably longer in the Militia and other second-line units. It was a good sturdy, well-made weapon. *Overall length 58.5 inches, barrel length 42 inches, calibre .75 (12 bore), weight 10 pounds 8 ounces.*

2 India Pattern firelock: Originally set up for the East India Company in 1760, this weapon saw some limited service with regular units serving in India before 1794. In February of that year the Company's Court of Directors authorised the transfer of a considerable quantity of its arms to the Board of Ordnance (28,920 firelocks in that year alone) and further purchases followed, both from the Company and directly from the trade until 1797 when it was adopted as standard in place of the more expensive Short Land Pattern.

Generally speaking it tends to be compared very unfavourably with the latter, but in fact it was in some ways superior. It was lighter, better balanced and the slightly shorter barrel helped speed up reloading - contemporary French firelocks had a barrel which was five inches longer. Set against these advantages was what was widely admitted to be a greatly inferior standard of workmanship, but this can be fairly attributed to the pressures of wartime manufacture rather than to any inherent design faults. At any rate the finish of post-war examples is markedly superior and despite

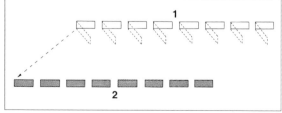

Dundas 13. March to a Flank in Echelon.

51

Prepare to Resist Cavalry – Ready. (Author)

the advent of the New Land Pattern it continued in service until the general adoption of percussion weapons in the 1840s. *Overall length 55.25 inches, barrel length 39 inches, calibre .75 (12 bore), weight 9 pounds 11 ounces.*

3 India Pattern locks. The original India Pattern lock was virtually identical to that previously used for Land Pattern weapons apart from some very minor cosmetic differences resulting from the more relaxed wartime acceptance standards. Previously engraved decoration for example was replaced by stamping. The only real change occurred in 1810 with the introduction of the ring-neck cock. In theory at least this was sturdier and cheaper than the traditional swan-neck style, but examples do exist of India Pattern weapons set up as late as the early part of Queen Victoria's reign with swan-neck cocks.

4. New Land Pattern lock. Although apparently cruder and much less elegant, the New Land Pattern lock was well designed and much sturdier than its predecessors. The question of which way up the flint should go was always a contentious issue and attracted a lengthy paragraph on the subject in the *Manual and Platoon Exercise* of 1834:

"In fixing flints, no uniform mode should be attempted; the flat side must be placed either upwards or downwards, according to the size and shape of the flint, and also according to the proportion which the cock bears in height to the hammer, which varies in different muskets; this is ascertained by letting the cock gently down, and observing where the flint strikes the hammer, which ought to be at the distance of one-third from the top of the hammer:- most diligent observation ought at the same time to be made whether every part of the edge of the flint comes in contact with the hammer, so as to strike out the fire from the whole surface... In whatever position the flint should be, it must be screwed in firmly and the cock should be let down, in order to observe whether the flint passes clear of the barrel."

5 New Land Pattern firelock. This pattern was introduced shortly after the Peace of Amiens in 1802, as a replacement for the old Short Land Pattern, but the resumption of hostilities with France saw production abandoned in favour of the less advanced but well established India Pattern. As a result only the Footguards and the 4th Foot were equipped with it. A light infantry variant was however ordered on the 28th October 1811 and by the end of the Peninsular War had been issued to the 43rd, 52nd, 68th, 71st and 85th light

Make Ready! In an important departure from previous drills, MacKenzie's platoon exercise for light infantry directed that firelocks should be cocked while levelled towards the enemy instead of being held vertically upright. This practice quickly spread and became mandatory for all regiments by 1828. (Author)

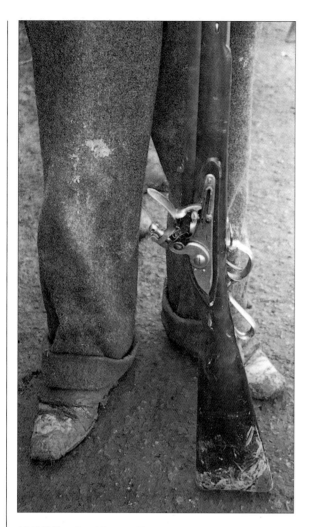

ABOVE **New Land Pattern Firelock for light infantry. (Author)**

talion's existence was spent on the march from one set of quarters to another. En route it would be accomodated each night, and on its twice weekly rest days, in civilian billets rather than in tented camps. When a unit was ordered on to the road its route and nightly halting places were specified in a Marching Order (normally referred to simply as a "Route") delivered to the officer commanding the battalion or detachment. Armed with this important document he could then legally demand billets, and 'diet and small beer' for himself, his men and of course their dependants, in any convenient Inns (or indeed anywhere else where alcohol could be bought), at those authorised halting places. The owner of the premises was of course compensated for this public service by a deduction from the soldier's subsistence, but as this charge was fixed annually by Parliament it might bear little relation to the actual cost.

infantry, as well as to those battalions of the 60th Foot not equipped with rifles. This variant featured a slightly shorter, browned, barrel, a rear-sight and trigger-guard. *New Land Pattern: Overall length 58.5 inches, barrel length 42 inches, calibre .75, weight 10 pounds 6 ounces.*
New Land Pattern light infantry: Overall length 55.5 inches, barrel length 39 inches, calibre .75, weight 10 pounds 1 ounce.
6 Land Pattern Bayonet 1760-80.
7 Land Pattern Bayonet 1780-1800.
8 India Pattern Bayonet 1787-1807.
9 India Pattern Bayonet (bearing East India Company marks) 1750-1805.
10 & 11 Bayonet scabbards used by 97th (Highland) Regiment c1795.
12 New Land Pattern ayonet sockets.

E: HALT ON THE MARCH

Despite the great barrack-building programme which began in 1793 neither regular nor militia units spent very much time in any one place. Consequently a considerable part of a bat-

ABOVE **Pile Arms after *Analytical View of the Manual and Platoon Exercises* by Captain Abraham Jones of the 67th Foot (Calcutta 1811). This usefully illustrates the uniform worn by British units in India at this time. Note the absence of lace except at the collar and the rather archaic cut of the jackets. The central soldier wears the regulation white breeches and black gaiters but the others wear white trousers and white gaiters.**

To help speed these unwelcome guests on their way, the Mutiny Act also provided for the issue of Warrants requiring the local authorities to provide "Carriages, with able Men to drive the same." Any carriage or wagon so impressed could only travel for one day's journey, sufficient it was assumed to take the regiment or company into somebody else's area. In the event of an officer detaining a wagon for a longer period, allowing any soldiers or women – other than the sick – to travel on it, or forcing the authorities "by Threatenings or menacing Words" to provide him with saddle horses, he was liable to be fined five pounds on each offence, the sum being deducted out of his pay.

This scene, based on a sketch by William Pyne, shows a typical change-over at an Inn, with baggage being unloaded from one such impressed wagon, before being reloaded onto another. A certain degree of informality is apparent and of particular interest is the woman with the baggage party, wearing a simple hooded poncho run up from an old blanket – a garment which can be seen in illustrations dating back to mediaeval times.

F: BARRACK ROOM LIFE

The Reay Fencibles, a home defence battalion, took up residence at Fort George Ardersier on the 10th of July 1795 and their regimental orders provide a very useful picture of barrack life. "*14th July:* The men to be up an hour before exercise, at which time their beds are to be turned up, blankets and sheets neatly folded, and the windows opened, that the rooms may be well aired... The barracks and passages to be constantly kept clean and swept."

Evidently they were not well enough swept, for next day the barracks were reported to be "in a very dirty state". Officers were to see that they were cleaned without delay and an inspection by the colonel himself was promised for the next day. In addition to the actual accommodation blocks the rest of the barracks had to be kept in good order as well. This was to be done every Thursday and Saturday with the Reay Fencibles being responsible for cleaning the north side and the Invalid company which formed the permanent garrison, looking after the south side. This was no doubt done then as now by forming a cordon to sweep through the allocated areas picking up any and all refuse by hand.

On the 23rd of July it was recommended that: "commanding officers of companies put the married people with their children in a room by themselves, in order that the men may not be disturbed by the noyse of the children. They are also to look for women cooks to cook the men's victuals, wash their linen, and keep their rooms and utensils in good order, which is always the custom in barracks, and adds much to the comfort and ease of the soldier..."

This plate is based on one of the restored barrack rooms at Fort George. Each room contained four double beds, a table, two benches, and a fireplace for cooking as well as warmth. If a battalion was fully recruited up to establishment overcrowding must have been severe, but in practice there was usually sufficient leeway to allow the allocation of rooms to families. Even if it did mean two or more families to one room it was still better than mixing them in with the unmarried men, and probably better too than what they might expect in civilian life. It is interesting to note from the

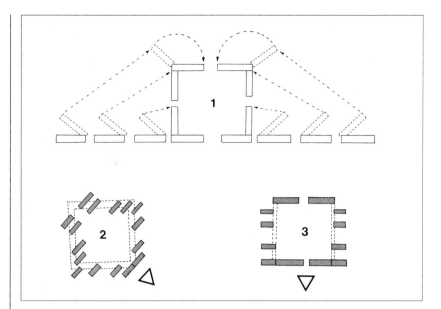

Dundas 14. **Hollow Square and its Movements. The two central companies stand fast while the outer ones backward wheel to the right and left and march into position as shown. Having formed square, the battalion was then required to move in various directions, which it does by facing subdivisions. The most important is the ability to move in echelon, since squares angled this way could create a crossfire and at the same time avoid shooting each other.**

Reays' orders however that the segregation of families from single men was done primarily in order that the latter could get an undisturbed night's sleep.

Children were evidently something of a problem for on the 17th of August the orders began with an instruction that, "no persons to bathe at or near the pier or landing-place of the ferry" just outside the fort and then went on to declare: "The sentries and soldiers on duty are to prevent the children in the garrison from throwing any stones, or in any respect defacing the barracks, or any other part of the buildings or works. If the children are found to persist in these wickednesses, they are to be brought to the officer of the main guard, who will order them to be confined in the Black Hole agreeable to the nature of their crime.

The wearing of civilian or "coloured" clothes in barracks was apparently quite common and the Reays' orders specifically allowed soldiers to wear "old clothes and old bonnets betwixt the hours of every parade, but not to go out of the garrison without being dressed as for parade, wearing their side arms..."

The trouble was finding somewhere to go. Fort George was, and still is, an unpopular posting and James Anton, then of the Aberdeenshire Militia, found it as bleak as everyone else who has ever had the great misfortune to serve there: "The Moray Firth washes three sides of the Fort, and on the other, the irreclaimable face of the country scarcely produces a blade of grass; furze bushes are thinly sprinkled over the rough stony moor, for upwards of a mile, in the direction of the small village of Campbelltown (Ardersier); but even to that place, inconsiderable as it was, we were not permitted to go, as it was beyond the prescribed limits. On purpose to evade this inhibition, some soldiers, of a regiment quartered in the Fort, lifted the milestone and placed it against the further end of the public-house in which they intended to regale themselves, and when they were brought back, and about to be tried for surpassing the limits prescribed for their perambulations, they pleaded that they had not gone beyond the milestone, and were pardoned; no doubt, more on account of the humour of the frolic than of the right to legal exculpation."

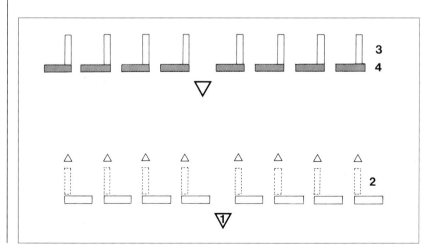

Dundas 15. **Retiring in Line and Firing. Having first retired a short distance in line, the companies form files to the right and retire. At a suitable distance the companies halt, about face and file back into line.**

G: LINE INFANTRY, ROYAL SCOTS C. 1800S

At the outbreak of war with France in 1793 the 1st or Royal Regiment of Foot had two battalions and by 1815 mustered no fewer than four. Between them they managed to be present in all major theatres of war. The First Battalion spent most of its time in the West Indies, but latterly served on the Canadian frontier. The Second Battalion was largely in the Mediterranean before being posted to India in 1807; the Third Battalion fought in the Peninsula and at Waterloo; while the Fourth Battalion served in North Germany, Holland, and Canada.

1 This reconstructed private wears the uniform pre-scribed in 1802, comprising the short-tailed jacket introduced in 1797, the cylindrical felt cap which replaced the old cocked hat in 1800, white breeches and black wool gaiters. Jackets had been widely worn as a comfortable and practical undress uniform, on campaign and in training, ever since the American War. As such they were quite plain and lacked tails (see **Plate B**), but when the old regimental coats were replaced in 1797 the elaborate regimental lace loopings were transferred from their lapels to the fronts of the new single-breasted jackets. As he would be promoted through the ranks so the rank chevrons, (**2**) inset along side him, would be awarded (top to bottom; Lance Corporal, Corporal, Sergeant, and Sergeant-Major). The wings on his shoulders identify him as a grenadier, men belonging to battalion com-panies simply had a white woollen tuft as shown in the inset (**3**). Such wings were normally made from red cloth but both the Royals and the Footguards regiments were allowed blue

ABOVE **The infantryman's view of the battlefield.**

ones as a mark of distinction. The soldier is further identified as a grenadier by the plain white plume on the front of his cap and the small grenade badge on the leather cockade. As a royal regiment the 1st were allowed their own badge (**4**) on the brass plate fronting their caps – (**5**) the standard version is also shown for comparison.

The soldier's accoutrements are substantially unchanged from those depicted in Plate B, with the exception of the knapsack (**6**). The envelope, (or Trotter) knapsack was introduced in 1805 for the light infantry reg-iments before seeing general adoption as late as 1812. Unlike the previous folding knapsack which had straps directly sewn to the material, the new style comprised a waterproofed canvas valise carried in quite separate buff leather slings. It was also blocked into shape by wooden boards, thus giving it a very smart appearance on parade - something which the Footguards are reliably said to have still been doing within living memory. On actual service, using the boards for firewood seems to have come under the heading of a time-honoured practice, and many period illustrations show the knapsack to be quite "soft" in appearance.

A much criticised feature of British knapsacks was the use of a breast-strap (**6a**) to adjust the fit by tightening or loosening the shoulder slings. If it were too tight the chest would be constricted, and if too loose, or even left undone, the slings would cut into the shoulder and affect circulation in the arms. In reality the problem was simply that too much

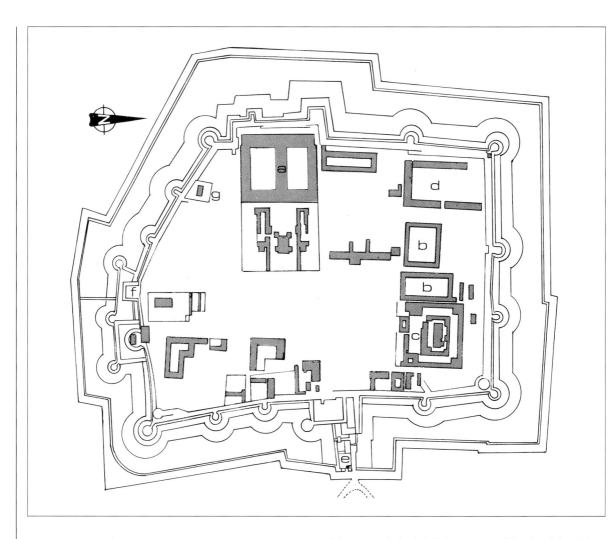

Vellore Fort 1806: (a) Palace of the Mysore Princes, (b) European Barracks, (c) Hindu Temple, (d) Officers' Quarters, (e) Arcot Gate, (f) Flagstaff Bastion, (g) Magazine.

weight was carried in the knapsack – a lesson which the British army's officers still have not learned at the present day. The solution then as now, was to quietly throw away all but the barest necessities and march with an empty or near-empty knapsack.

The regimental number was to be painted in white on the outer face of the knapsack (**6b**) (the flap providing access to the contents formed the inner face) and this particular inscription is taken from a painting by Dennis Dighton depicting the storming of San Sebastian in 1813. The same illustration shows that the blue painted wooden canteen bore the similar inscription *3 Battn/Royal/Scots*. Other items shown are **7** pocket knife; **8** musket tool; **9** breast plate of 3rd Battalion; **10** breastplate of 1st Battalion; **11** officer's breastplate and how it attached to belt.

H: 69TH FOOT AT VELLORE

In July 1806 four companies of the 1/69th Foot, totalling some 390 rank and file besides officers, were stationed at

Vellore, a substantial fortress some 80 miles inland from Madras, together with the 1/1 Native Infantry and 2/23rd Native Infantry. Just after 12 o'clock on the night of the 10th of July both Sepoy regiments mutinied and attempted to seize the fort, presumably with the intention of releasing the sons of Tipoo Sahib who were imprisoned in the palace. The mutineers' first target, naturally enough, was the Arcot Gate and the guardroom of the 69th, but although all or most of the soldiers there that night were killed, the guard commander, Sergeant Peter Brady escaped, roused the men in their barracks and held off the initial attempt to rush them. Thus thwarted the mutineers rampaged through the rest of the fort killing twelve of their own officers and all the other Europeans they could find, although there are conflicting reports as to whether women and children were amongst their number.

Under cover of the confusion a handful of 69th officers (many of them were sleeping outside the fort and so took no part in the action) managed to reach the barracks only to find when they got there that their surviving men had very few cartridges in their possession. Moreover the mutineers had managed to bring up two light field guns and were rapidly knocking the barracks to pieces, so Captain Archibald

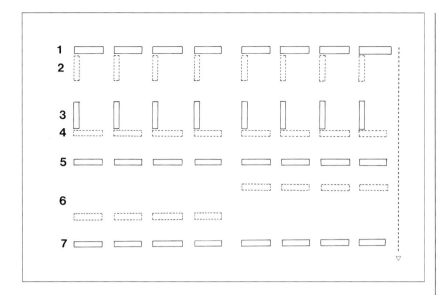

Dundas 16. **Advancing in Line, Filing, Charging to the Front. This begins as a reversal of the previous exercise, forming and advancing in files then deploying into line, after which, in a very modern looking example of fire and manoeuvre, the two wings give each other covering fire while alternately advancing in short tactical bounds, before reforming line, firing a volley and charging.**

MacLachlan led about 200 men in a breakout on to the north wall of the fort. There for a time they held out in one of the bastions, but as it was overlooked from a large pagoda, MacLachlan then decided to move further along the ramparts in order to reach the less exposed north-east angle bastion. Almost at once he was shot and wounded, but Captain Charles Barrow took over and pushed on down the east wall as far as the top of the Arcot Gate. There they were relatively secure, but by now desperately short of ammunition. Barrow therefore set off with some 60 men to try and reach an isolated magazine by the south-west wall. He too was shot and "dangerously wounded" at the outset. All of the other officers were either dead, wounded or skulking by this time, but Sergeant Brady took command and fought his way through to the magazine, only to discover that it had already been looted. Undaunted he formed his men up again and retraced his steps back to the gate, stopping en route while Sergeant John McManus and Private Philip Bottom climbed up a flagpole under heavy fire and appropriated the Mysore standard which the mutineers had raised on the flagstaff bastion.

Meanwhile the detachment's commander, Major Richard Coates, who had been sleeping in a bungalow outside the fort, despatched a messenger to Arcot, summoning the 19th Light Dragoons. As it happened he arrived just as they were falling in for morning parade and their commanding officer, Colonel Rollo Gillespie, mounted them up and led them straight up the road to Vellore. Unfortunately, although the surviving men, women and children of the 69th (and their colours) were still esconced on top of the Arcot Gate when he got there, the gate itself was firmly barred and still in the possession of the mutineers. Undismayed, Gillespie, who by a curious co-incidence had met Sergeant Brady while they were both serving on San Domingo ten years before, got himself hauled up by a makeshift rope cobbled together from cross-belts. The actual gates themselves were quickly blown in by Gillespie's two curricle guns, but as the Sepoys still blocked the angled passageway within, Gillespie and Brady mustered the exhausted remnants of the 69th and cleared it with a bayonet charge. No-one was in any mood for taking

prisoners by this time and the dragoons are said to have herded the greater part of the mutineers into a confined space between the pagoda and the east wall and there blown apart with canister fire.

In six hours of fighting the 69th had lost three officers killed and three wounded, along with four sergeants, four corporals, one drummer and 75 privates killed while another 91 of all ranks (possibly including some of the officers belonging to the 1/1st and 2/23rd N.I.) were wounded, some of them seriously. Each of the four companies seems to have lost about the same number: Captain Marc Rene Montalambert's Company had Sergeant William Caseman and 20 privates killed out of 90; Captain Henry de la Douespe's Company lost Sergeant Edward Rawson, corporals William Job and Isaac Short, Drummer Robert King and 18 privates killed out of 85; Captain Charles Barrow's Company had sergeants John Gibbons and John Shaw killed, corporals Joseph Adams and John Walker and 19 privates killed out of 89; Captain Archibald MacLachlan's Company escaped most lightly, with only 17 privates killed out of 79.

Although Sergeant Peter Brady's part in the action was virtually written out of the story by Victorian historians who preferred that their heroes should be officers, (the fact that most of the officers were elsewhere was also an embarrassment) it was well recognised at the time. He was initially given an Ensign's commission in the 12th Foot at nearby Seringapatam, but instead transferred to the East India Company's service as a Conductor in the Ordnance Department at Fort St.George Madras. In both cases his commission was dated to the 10th of July 1806 - the date on which he had earned it the hard way. After service with the Nizam of Hyderabad's Subsidiary Force between 1814 and 1817 he was promoted to Lieutenant in the Carnatic European Battalion in 1819, transferring three years later to a Lieutenancy in the 2nd Native Veteran Battalion, before dying at Madras on the 24th September 1824.

I: FOOTWEAR

In theory each man should have had two pairs of shoes in his

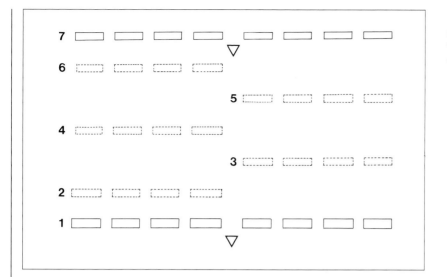

possession, although active service could usually make a mockery of this. Army shoes were made on straight lasts and it was invariably recommended that they should change feet on a daily basis in order to prevent them "running crooked". Although allowing them to mould on to particular feet (ie; forming right and left) was much more comfortable it was reckoned to weaken the shoe by straining both leather and stitching. Oddly enough the same advice was still being given out by the powers that be in respect of socks as late as 1914.

The most frequent complaints about the ammunition boot concerned its distressing tendency to fall apart very quickly - some contractors provided shoes which were only glued, not sewn together. Each battalion therefore carried a number of cobblers on its strength. Like the tailors these men (known as "handicrafts") were mustered as ordinary soldiers but allowed to charge for their services according to an officially regulated scale. Although he may thereby have escaped some of the unpleasanter jobs, being a company cobbler was not altogether an unmixed blessing, not least because he was expected to carry all the leather and tools he required in addition to his normal kit.

Landing in the Peninsula in August 1808 Rifleman Benjamin Harris complained: "The weight I myself toiled under was tremendous... for besides my well-filled kit (knapsack), there was the greatcoat rolled on its top, my blanket and camp kettle, my haversack, stuffed full of leather for repairing the men's shoes, together with a hammer and other tools (the lapstone I took the liberty of flinging to the devil), ship-biscuit and beef for three days. I also carried my canteen filled with water, my hatchet and rifle, and eighty rounds of ball cart-ridge in my pouch."

Without the lapstone -a two-piece last designed to sit on the cobbler's lap, instead of a bench - there was very little which Harris could do in the way of repairing shoes on his own, and his practice thereafter was simply to take over the local cobbler's shop whenever his company stopped. This expedient was obviously much more sensible than carrying around a heavy cast-iron lapstone, on top of his other accoutrements, and probably a very widespread practice throughout the time they were in use.

Seen alonside this figure (**1**) working on his lapstone are; **2** exploded view of a typical shoe worn by infantrymen of the period and **2a** the basic leather fabric cut for it's construction; **3a** two-piece cast iron lapstone, and (**3b**) when fitted together for use; **4** laced shoes more commonly worn on campaign than buckled ones; **5** straight lasted military shoes with **5a** exploded view of buckle, and (**5b**) how it looked once attached to the fabric of the shoe.

J: 79TH HIGHLANDERS AT WATERLOO

The 79th (Cameron) Highlanders fought at Waterloo in Sir James Kempt's 8th Infantry Brigade, comprising the 28th, 32nd and 79th Foot and the 1/95th Rifles. At the outset of the campaign the ten companies of the regiment mustered 758 officers and men, besides a further 15 officers and NCOs making up the regimental staff. The companies had obviously been "equalised" before proceeding on active service, in order to serve as platoons, for three of the battalion companies comprised 68, 65 and 69 officers and men apiece, while the others had between 72 and 76. As usual the two flank companies were appreciably stronger with the grenadiers mustering 92 officers and men and the light infantry 94.

A useful account of the regiment's part in the opening stages of the battle is provided in a letter written by Private Alexander Cruickshank of the light company:

"When the 79th were deploying into line at the commencement of the Action (they having been previously in column) the Light Company, to which I then belonged, were ordered out and extended. On our reaching the hedge (or nearly so), where the Guns were stationed, we passed through the Belgian Infantry, who were retiring, and pushed down the slope in front of the hedge into the valley, where we were for some time engaged with the French skirmishers; but a strong Column of the Enemy appearing on the top of the opposite ridge immediately in our front, and a second Column was at that moment seen advancing along the valley to our left, which must have come into contact with the 28th Regiment, we were consequently obliged to retire, and joined the Regiment on its reaching the hedge, when a tremendous conflict ensued between our Line and the

Highland troops sketched in Paris in 1815; although the two men on the left have no tapes on their arms, the fact that they are both wearing sashes suggests that they may in fact be sergeants. (NMS)

opposing Columns, which, it has been said, pushed themselves so far forward as to reach the hedge; but I can positively assert that the French did not reach that point, if I except indeed some few of their sharpshooters which came up the hill with the light infantry, but were quickly driven back."

Like many other units by this time the 79th Highlanders could deploy rather more than a single company of skirmishers if the need arose, and Lieutenant Alexander Forbes of No.1 Company recalled that at Quatre Bras two days earlier: "Our ground had scarcely been thus occupied when the Enemy's advance appeared. The Light Companies of the 8th Brigade, to which were added the 8th Company and marksmen of the 79th Regiment, were immediately thrown out, when the Action commenced."

The employment of No.8 company as skirmishers may well have been a long-standing practice for a Lieutenant Kevan Leslie afterwards declared that he had belonged to the regiment's Light Company at Waterloo, yet the regimental rolls show him to have actually served in No.8 Company. At any rate its employment as skirmishers may help to account for a curious anomaly in the casualty returns. Out of 69 officers and men serving in the company at the commencement of the three days of fighting, only 14 including Lieutenant Leslie were unhurt by the end of it. As

for the others, 16 were dead or would die of their wounds, another 16 were badly hurt but would survive, and no fewer than 23 officers and men were returned as slightly wounded. Most of the other companies tended to return an average of 7 slightly wounded, and although there were some with more, none approached No.8 Company's total. In contrast the other companies consistently returned a higher proportion of men fit for duty and it may simply mean that minor injuries were less commonly reported in those companies.

There were, however, some other differences which are less easily explained. The grenadier company for example suffered far more casualties than any other, with 23 killed or died of their wounds, 38 badly wounded and eight slightly wounded out of 92 – all the officers and sergeants being killed or wounded. On the other hand No.1 Company, which probably stood next to the grenadiers, had only 7 dead, 17 badly wounded and 15 slightly wounded out of 68. Oddly enough all the officers were wounded in this company, but none of the sergeants were hit.

All in all the battles of Quatre Bras and Waterloo cost the 79th Highlanders 8 officers, 5 sergeants and 90 rank & file dead, 23 officers, 21 sergeants and 309 men wounded, and one man, Private Neil Turner of No.3 Company, taken prisoner.

K: PIONEER 21ST FOOT, 1815

1 The 21st Royal Scots Fusiliers saw comparatively little active service during this period apart from a spell in the West Indies during the 1790s. They then spent some time in various Mediterranean garrisons where discipline seems to

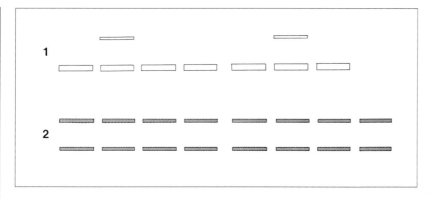

Dundas 18. **Advancing in Line. The grand finale of any review in which the battalion advances in line, halting twice to fire volleys obliquely to the right and left. Note how the light infantry company is deployed in one rank behind each flank, keeping out of the way until required to skirmish. At the end, the company forms on the left flank and the battalion opens its ranks to open order.**

have suffered, but in 1814/5 however they fought at Bladensburg and New Orleans.

Each company in a battalion contributed two men to the pioneer section, under the command of a corporal. No special badges were worn – apart from the plate on the front of the bearskin cap prescribed for home service (**2**) – and the wings on this man's shoulders show that he belongs to the grenadier company. Pioneers drawn from the eight battalion companies would just wear the usual worsted tufts. The grey trousers shown were only supposed to be worn on active service, but by this period it was probably rare to see white breeches and black gaiters except on the most formal of occasions. The short grey gaiters worn underneath the trousers were to be made from the same material.

On active service the usual cap or shako was worn and in theory at least the principal distinction of the pioneer was his beard. The wearing of a beard was a privilege which reflected the fact that forming the advance party on a march usually entailed setting off before dawn and shaving in the dark was hardly a practical proposition. Like so many other privileges in the army however, it soon became a requirement and even today it is still expected of the regimental pioneer sergeant that he will grow a suitably impressive beard. In practice however beards were probably much more widely worn on active service than contemporary illustrations suggest. William Lawrence of the 40th recalled that when he served under General Auchmuty during the attempt on Buenos Aires in 1807: "We thought Sir Samuel Auchmuty an excellent commander... Although the fashion at that time was for soldiers to be smart, with long powdered hair, Sir Samuel believed they should be rough-looking, with long beards and greasy haversacks. It was because of his dislike of dandyism that the fashion for powdered hair was done away with soon after we landed in South America. Of course, it might have been that it was difficult to get the powder." In the Peninsula, under Wellington, beards were probably just as common - though not moustaches, except perhaps in some cavalry regiments. Indeed given the well documented tendency for British soldiers to sieze any excuse to wear beards on active service throughout the 19th century it would perhaps be rather odd if it was otherwise in the Peninsula.

As for the specialist equipment, the official scale for each battalion, on Home Service at least, was 11 bearskin caps, 11 calfskin knapsacks, 11 leather aprons, 11 pouches, 11 firelock slings, 11 breastplates, 11 bill-hooks with cases and girdles and 11 firelocks. The calfskin knapsacks were slung from a single strap on the right hip in order to allow the larger

tools such as axes or saws to be carried on the back in place of the ordinary knapsack. The mention of (ammunition pouches, and breastplates without any reference being made to cross-belts is probably an oversight as these items are in fact shown in contemporary illustrations of pioneers.

A typical selection of tools is shown, together with some of the smaller and more mundane items of soldiers' kit: pioneer knapsack and contents, **3a** brushes, **3b** D section mess tin, **3c** twisted wire fork, **3d** horn spoon, **3e** soap dish (probably only used in barracks), **3f** shaving brush and cut throat razor, **3g** bone-handled toothbrush, and **3h** wooden button-stick. Other items seen are; **4** saw and carrying case **5** bill hook and case, and, **6** heavy tools.

L: AFTER THE WARS

Quartermaster-Sergeant James Anton concluded his narrative of service in the 42nd Highlanders by saying "I am now about to proceed to Chelsea." The Royal Hospital at Chelsea was founded by Charles II in 1682 in order to provide for wounded and disabled soldiers. Within a few months of its actual opening 10 years later all of the places were filled, and a system of 'Out-Pensions' was instituted to provide some financial relief for those soldiers who could not be accommodated as 'In-Pensioners'. From the 1750s length of service could also entitle a soldier to be admitted to pension although it appears from the registers that this merely regularised an existing situation whereby very old soldiers could be admitted simply on the grounds of their being "worn-out".

Having been discharged a soldier would make his way to Chelsea in order to be assessed to pension, a process vividly described by Sergeant William Lawrence of the 40th: "We marched to Leith, embarked on the Leith packet and, after some very rough weather, landed at Gravesend. We moved on to Chatham where we remained for six weeks waiting to pass the board. We re-embarked on a small craft at Gravesend and went up river to the Tower of London. From there we marched to Chelsea Hospital.

"The next morning, we were examined by the doctor and then called up before the board, one at a time. When it was my turn, I was asked my age and length of service. One of the gentlemen called out 'Seven!' but the doctor immediately said 'Nine!' because of the wound in my knee. This meant I should receive a pension of ninepence a day for that was what was settled on me for life. I went to an office, where I received my expenses to Dorchester - one shilling and tenpence for myself, and three-halfpence for my wife, for every ten miles."

As Lawrence indicates, the actual pension paid could vary according to the soldier's age, length of service, "character" and any wounds or disability. Three years earlier Private Josh Prettibier of the 6th Foot appeared before the board and was awarded one shilling and thruppence a day on the strength of his 27 years service and the fact that at 45 he was "worn out". Providing he did not disqualify himself by bad conduct or self-inflicted disabilities induced by syphilis or alcohol (and thus brought beggary upon himself), the level of Out-Pension was assessed by way of a supplement to whatever income the discharged soldier could reasonably expect to earn in civilian life. Places in Chelsea Hospital itself appear to have been reserved for those soldiers so worn out or disabled as to be quite incapable of work.

Those thus admitted were provided with food, accommodation, and a small allowance, together with the Chelsea Hospital uniform depicted here. Originally the same uniform was worn by the sedentary battalions and Independent Companies of Invalids, but the short-lived veteran battalions which replaced them wore the ordinary infantry uniform.

A second Royal Hospital existed (and indeed pre-dated the Chelsea one) at Kilmainham in Ireland. Prior to the Union in 1801 this establishment accomodated In-Pensioners and provided Out-Pensions for soldiers discharged from regiments assigned to the then quite separate Irish establishment, irrespective of the geographical origins of those soldiers. Responsibility for the payment of all Out-Pensions transferred to Chelsea in 1822 and generally speaking admission as In-Pensioners to Kilmainham seems to have been restricted to Irishmen after that date.

Out-Pensions could also be awarded to veterans of the Kings German Legion and some other foreign units in British pay, but in these cases there was no entitlement to a place as an In-Pensioner.

Notes sur les planches en couleur

A Bien que la méthode de recrutement traditionnelle au roulement de tambour fut utilisée durant toute la période couverte par cette étude, on autorisa et même encouragea des miliciens en nombre considérable à se porter volontaires pour servir dans l'armée. D'ordinaire, les lois de la Milice interdisaient cette pratique et il fallut passer des lois spéciales pour l'autoriser à certaines dates. Pour commencer, on utilisa cette technique peu souvent et les premières lois de ce type furent adopt en 1798 et 1799. Mais à partir de 1805, cett pratique se généralisa et se transforma en un processus annuel dès 1807.

B1 Ce soldat porte l'uniforme d'un confort surprenant que les troupes étaient autorisées à porter pendant leur service aux Antilles à partir de 1790. Ce personnage spécifique est dépeint en uniforme de marche complet, composé de **2** un havresac pliant en toile pour transporter des vêtements de rechange, **3** intérieur de la cartouchière montrant comment elle était rattachée aux bandoulières croisées beiges, **4** boucle en crin et cuivre, **5** cartouche et moule **6** cantine à eau en bois de deux quarts, **7** havresac en lin **8** brosse et pic **9** étui à fifre en cuivre **10** Couvre-fusilet **11** couvre-canon en bois **12** Bouton de régiment.

C Cette planche décrit un moment typique de la formation de l'infanterie légère. Deux soldats, un caporal et un autre homme expérimenté démontrent l'art de l'escarmouche, sous les ordres d'un sergent tiré aux quatre épingles. Le caporal vise une cible imaginaire alors qu'il est couvert par un soldat derrière lui. Lorsque le caporal a tiré, son partenaire s'avancera de six pieds pour passer devant lui pendant qu'il recharge son arme.

D1 Pistolet à fusil court modèle Land. **2** Pistolet à fusil modèle India **3** Fusils modèle India **4** Fusil nouveau modèle India. **5** Pistolet à fusil nouveau modèle Land. **6** Baïonnette modèle Land 1760-80. **7** Baïonnette modèle Land 1780-1800. **8** Baïonnette modèle India 1787-1807. **9** Baïonnette modèle India (qui porte les marques de la East India Company) 1750-1805. **10 & 11** Fourreaux de baïonnette utilisés par le 97e Régiment (Highland) vers 1795. **12** Porte-baïonnette nouveau modèle Land.

E Malgré le grand programme de construction de casernes qui débuta en 1793, les unités régulières et celles de milice ne passaient pas beaucoup de temps au même endroit. Par conséquent, une partie considérable de l'existence d'un bataillon se passait en marche, d'un baraquement à l'autre. En route, le bataillon logeait chaque nuit, et deux fois par semaine lors de ses jours de repos, dans des cantonnements civils plutôt que dans des camps, sous la tente.

F Cette planche s'inspire d'une caserne restaurée de Fort George. Chaque chambre contenait quatre grands lits, une table, deux bancs et une cheminée pour la cuisine et le chauffage. Si un bataillon était complet, les logements devaient être surpeuplés, mais en pratique, il existait suffisamment de marge pour autoriser l'attribution de certaines chambres à des familles. Même si cela signifiait que deux familles ou plus devaient partager une chambre, c'était mieux que de les mêler aux hommes célibataires et, sans doute mieux que ce qu'ils auraient trouvé dans la vie civile.

G1 Uniforme prescrit en 1802, **2** Rangs de sous-officiers (de haut en bas: Caporal, Caporal, Sergent et Sergent-Major). Les galons de ses épaules indiquent qu'il s'agit d'un grenadier. Les hommes appartenant aux compagnies d'un bataillon avaient simplement une huppe en laine blanche comme illustré en encadré **3**. En tant que régiment royal, le 1st était autorisé à avoir son propre badge **4** à la plaque de cuivre à l'avant de leur calot. **5** la version standard est également reproduite pour permettre les comparaisons. **6** Havresac "Trotter", introduit en 1805 pour les régiments d'infanterie légère avant d'être adopté par tous en 1812 seulement. Le numéro du régiment devait être peint en blanc sur l'extérieur du havresac **6b**. Les autres objets représentés sont **7** un couteau pliant **8** un outil de mousquet **9** le plastron du 3e bataillon **10** le plastron du 1er bataillon **11** plastron d'officier et méthode de fixation à la ceinture.

H En six heures de combat, les 69e Fantassins avaient perdu 3 officiers et 3 autres furent blessés, ainsi que quatre sergents, quatre caporaux, un tambour et 75 simples soldats tués, plus 91 hommes de tous rangs (y compris peut-être certains officiers appartenant au 1/1er et 2/23e N.I.) furent blessés, certains grièvement. Chacune des quatre compagnies semble avoir perdu le même nombre d'hommes.

I En théorie, chaque homme devait avoir deux paires de chaussures mais en pratique, ceci n'était jamais le cas. Les chaussures de l'armée étaient fabriquées sur des formes droites et on recommandait toujours de changer de pied tous les jours pour éviter aux chaussures de se déformer. Permettre aux chaussures de se mouler à un pied spécifique (le gauche ou le droit) aurait été bien plus confortable mais on pensait que cela affaiblissait la chaussure en forçant sur le cuir et sur les coutures. Bizarrement, les mêmes conseils étaient donnés concernant les chaussettes jusqu'en 1914.

J Les 79e Highlanders (Cameron) se battirent à Waterloo dans la 8e Brigade d'Infanterie de Sir James Kempt, qui comprenait les 28e, 32e et 79e Fantassins et les 1/95e Fusiliers. Dès le début de la campagne, les dix compagnies du régiment rassemblèrent 758 officiers et hommes en plus de 15 officiers et sous-officiers supplémentaires qui constituaient l'état-major du régiment.

K1 Les 21e Fusiliers Royal Scots furent relativement peu actifs durant cette période, à l'exception d'une période aux Antilles vers 1790. Ils ne portaient aucun badge spécial, à part la plaque sur le devant du bonnet à poil prescrite pour le service national **2** - et les galons sur les épaules de cet homme montrent qu'il appartient à une compagnie de grenadiers. Les pionniers extraits des huit compagnies du bataillon portaient les huppes de worsted habituelles. La culotte grise illustrée ici devait uniquement être portée durant le service actif mais à cette époque, il était sans doute rare de voir une culotte blanche et des guêtres noires, sauf durant les plus grandes occasions. **3** havresac de pionnier et son contenu a brosses, **3b** gamelle en D, **3c** fourchette en fil tordu, **3d** cuillère en corne, **3e** porte-savon (sans doute utilisé seulement en caserne), **3f** blaireau et rasoir, **3g** brosse a dents en os et, **3h** crochet à boutons en bois. Les autres objets sont **4** scie et son coffret; serpette et son coffet et **5** gros outils.

L Le Commissaire-Sergent James Anton termina son récit de service dans les 42e Highlanders en déclarant "je suis maintenant prêt à partir pour Chelsea". L'Hôpital Royal de Chelsea fut fondé par Charles II en 1682 afin de loger les soldats blessés et handicapés. Quelques mois après son ouverture, 10 ans plus tard, toutes les places étaient prises et un système de "pensionnaires externes" fut mis en place afin de fournir une aide financière aux soldats qui ne pouvaient venir vivre sur place.

Farbtafeln

A Zwar ging man während der hier in Betracht gezogenen Zeit der herkömmlichen Art und Weise der Rekrutierung - nämlich per Trommelschlag - nach, doch wurden etliche Mitglieder der Bürgerwehr freigestellt, wenn nicht sogar aufgefordert, sich freiwillig zum Heer zu melden. Normalerweise untersagten die Verordnungen der Bürgerwehr genau dieses Vorgehen, und es wurden eigens Gesetze notwendig, um eine Genehmigung zu erlangen. Zunächst griff man auf solche Maßnahmen nur selten zurück, und die ersten derartigen Gesetze wurden 1798 und 1799 erlassen. Ab 1805 geschah dies jedoch häufiger, bis es von 1807 an schließlich zu einem alljährlichen Unterfangen wurde.

B1 Dieser Soldat trägt die erstaunlich bequeme Uniform, die ab 1790 an Truppen für den Dienst auf den Westindischen Inseln ausgegeben wurde. Die Figur ist in der kompletten Marschordnung abgebildet, die aus folgenden Elementen besteht: **2** faltbarer Rucksack aus Segeltuch für Kleidungsstücke zum Wechseln; **3** Innenansicht der Patronentasche, die zeigt, wie sie an den Kreuzriemen aus weißem Büffelleder befestigt war; **4** Roßhaar-Unterlage und Messingschnalle; **5** Patrone und Falzer; **6** Feldflasche aus Holz für 2 Quarts Flüssigkeit; **7** Brotbeutel aus Leinen; **8** Bürste und Picker; **9** Pfeifenetui aus Messing; **10** Schloßdeckel; **11** hölzerner Mündungspropfen; **12** Regimentsknopf.

C Auf dieser Farbtafel ist ein typischer Augenblick bei der Ausbildung der Leichten Infanterie festgehalten. Zwei Soldaten, ein Obergefreiter und ein weiterer erfahrener Recke, demonstrieren die Kunst des Plänkelns unter der Regie eines tadellos angezogenen Feldwebels. Der Obergefreite legt auf ein hypothetisches Ziel an, während ihm sein Mannschaftssoldat von hinten Deckung gibt. Hat der Obergefreite erst einmal gefeuert, so begibt sich sein Partner bis zu sechs Schritte vor ihn, während er neu lädt.

D1 Short Land Pattern-Muskete. **2** India Pattern-Muskete. **3** India Pattern-Zündschlösser. **4** Neues Land Pattern-Zündschloß. **5** Neue Land Pattern-Muskete. **6** Land Pattern-Bajonett, 1760-80. **7** Land Pattern-Bajonett, 1780-1800. **8** India Pattern-Bajonett, 1787-1807. **9** India Pattern-Bajonett (mit dem Zeichen der East India Company), 1750-1805. **10 & 11** Bajonettscheiden, wie sie das 97th (Highland) Regiment um 1795 benutzte. **12** Neue Land Pattern-Bajonettlager.

E Trotz des großangelegten Bauprogramms für Kasernen, das 1793 in Angriff genommen wurde, verbrachten weder die Einheiten der Miliz je lange Zeit an einem Ort. Folglich spielte sich der Großteil des Lebens eines Bataillons auf dem Marsch von einem Quartier zum anderen ab. Unterwegs wurde für Unterkunft gesorgt, und zwar stellte man die Soldaten abends und an den Ruhetagen zweimal in der Woche statt in Zeltlagern privat einquartiert.

F Diese Abbildung beruht auf einem der restaurierten Kasernenräume im Fort George. In den Räumen standen jeweils vier Doppelbetten, ein Tisch, zwei Bänke, und es gab ein Kamin zum Kochen und Heizen. Falls ein Bataillon bis zur vollen Truppenstärke rekrutiert war, so mußten die Räumlichkeiten sehr überfüllt gewesen sein, in der Praxis gab es jedoch meist genügend Spielraum, um die Räume je nach Familien einzuteilen. Mußten sich dabei zwei oder mehr Familien in einem Zimmer wohnten, so war dies immer noch eine bessere Lösung, als sie zusammen mit ledigen Soldaten unterzubringen. Unter Umständen waren die Bedingungen auch besser, als die Zustände, mit denen sie im zivilen Leben rechnen mußten.

G1 Uniform, die 1802 vorgeschrieben wurde. **2** Unteroffiziersränge (von oben nach unten: Hauptgefreiter, Obergefreiter, Feldwebel, Hauptfeldwebel). Die Flügel auf den Schultern machen ihn als Grenadier erkenntlich. Soldaten, die Bataillonskompanien angehörten, hatten einfach eine weiße Quaste aus Wolle, wie auf dem kleinen Bild gezeigt **3**. Als königlichem Regiment stand dem 1st ein eigenes Abzeichen auf der Messingplatte auf der Vorderseite der Mütze zu - **5** zum Vergleich ist auch die Standardversion abgebildet. **6** "Trotter"-Rucksack, der 1805 für die Regimenter der Leichten Infanterie eingeführt wurde, bis er erst 1812 allgemein Verwendung fand. Die Regimentsnummer sollte in Weiß auf die äußere Hülle des Rucksacks gemalt werden **6b**. Bei den weiteren Gegenständen handelt es sich um: **7** Taschenmesser; **8** Musketenwerkzeug; **9** Brustplatte des 3. Bataillons; **10** Brustplatte des 1. Bataillons; **11** Offiziersbrustplatte und deren Befestigung am Gürtel.

H Im sechsstündigen Gefecht waren beim 69th drei Offiziere gefallen und drei verwundet, desweiteren fielen vier Feldwebel, vier Obergefreite, ein Trommler und 75 Gefreite, und 91 Männer aller Ränge (darunter möglicherweise einige der Offiziere des 1/1st und 2/23rd N.I.) wurden verwundet, manche trugen schwere Verletzungen davon. Jede der vier Kompanien scheint etwa gleich große Verluste erlitten zu haben.

I Theoretisch hätte jeder Soldat zwei Paar Schuhe besitzen sollen, was sich im aktiven Dienst in der Tat als graue Theorie herausstellte. Die Schuhe für das Heer wurden auf einem geraden Leisten gefertigt. Es wurde den Männern stets nahegelegt, die Schuhe täglich jeweils am anderen Fuß zu tragen, damit diese nicht "krumm laufen". Zwar waren die Schuhe viel bequemer, wenn man sie immer am gleichen Fuß trug, so daß sie sich dem Fußform anpassen konnten (d.h. ein rechter und ein linker Schuh wurden). Man war jedoch der Ansicht, ein solches Vorgehen würde den Schuh schwächen, da sowohl das Leder als auch die Nähte strapaziert werden. Seltsamerweise erteilte man sogar noch 1914 für Socken ähnliche Ratschläge.

J Die 79th (Cameron) Highlanders kämpften bei Waterloo in Sir James Kempt's 8th Infantry Brigade, die sich aus den 28th, 32nd und 79th Foor und der 1/95th Rifles zusammensetzte. Bei Beginn des Feldzuges boten die zehn Kompanien des Regiments 758 Offiziere und Mannschaften auf, daneben stellten weitere 15 Offiziere und Unteroffiziere den Regimentsstab.

K1 Die 21st Royal Scots Fusiliers wurden während vom Einsatz auf den Westindischen Inseln in den 90er Jahren des 18. Jahrhunderts in dieser Epoche kaum zum aktiven Dienst herangezogen. Man trug keine besonderen Abzeichen - außer der Platte auf der Vorderseite der Bärenfellmütze, die für den Dienst in der Heimat vorgeschriebene war **2** - und den Flügeln auf den Schultern der abgebildeten Figur, die erkenntlich machen, daß er der Grenadierkompanie angehört. Pioniere aus den acht Bataillonskompanien trugen einfach die üblichen Quasten aus Kammgarn. Die abgebildeten grauen Hosen sollten eigentlich nur im aktiven Dienst getragen werden, doch sah man in dieser Epoche weiße Breeches und schwarze Gamaschen oder bei ganz formellen Anlässen wahrscheinlich nur noch selten. **3** Pionier-Rucksack und Inhalt: **3a** Bürsten; **3b** Kochgeschirr; **3c** Gabel aus Draht; **3d** Hornlöffel; **3e** Seifenschale (wurde wahrscheinlich nur in der Kaserne benutzt); **3f** Rasierpinsel und Rasiermesser; **3g** Zahnbürste mit Knochengriff; **3h** Knopfhaken aus Holz. Bei den anderen abgebildeten Gegenständen handelt es sich um eine Säge mit Tragtasche **4** und schwere Werkzeuge **5**.

L Quartiermeister-Feldwebel James Anton schloß seine Schilderung des Dienstes bei den 42th Highlanders mit den Worten ab: "Nun begab ich mich nach Chelsea." Das Royal Hospital in Chelsea wurde 1682 von Charles II. gegründet, und für verwundete und behinderte Soldaten zu sorgen. Nur wenige Monate nach der eigentlichen Eröffnung zehn Jahre später waren alle Plätze besetzt, und es mußten "externe Renten" eingeführt werden, um denjenigen Soldaten, für die als "interne Rentner" kein Platz war, finanzielle Hilfe leisten zu können.